NMLS SAFE

Study Guide

2023-2024

Pass the Mortgage Loan Originator Test - Fast and Easy!

420+ Practice Questions with Answers!

Richard R. Barkley

Russell Jordan

CSB ACADEMY PUBLISHING CO.

COVER DESIGN

BY

JESSICA ALBRIGHT

FIRST EDITION

Contents

Chapter 1: Real Estate Vocabulary

The world of real estate is much bigger than the term "mortgage" itself. One of the key reasons consumers encounter difficulties with buying or selling a home is that they lack the proper terminology. Anyone taking the NMLS exam must know the essential real estate terms listed in this chapter. Pay attention to the numbers as they are often asked in the exam. <u>All important points that appear on the exam have been underlined.</u>

Acceleration clause: Also referred to as the 'acceleration covenant,' is a provision in the contract. It will state that the borrower will have to repay all his or her outstanding loans to the lender if specific requirements established by the lender are not met.

Active contingent: When a potential home buyer makes an offer on a home, the offer is usually contingent upon the buyer being able to meet certain conditions before the sale can be finalized. Common contingencies include receiving approval for the mortgage, the buyer being able to sell his or her home, or coming to an agreement with the seller on details of the home inspection.

Active under contract: Sometimes the seller will accept an offer for the home from a buyer with contingencies but at the same time would like the home to be actively listed, this is known as 'active under contract.' In such scenarios, the seller wants to ensure that he has backup offers in case the current buyer's offer fails to meet the contingencies.

Addendum: If a buyer or seller wants to change an existing contract, they can add an addendum outlining the specific portion of the contract they would like to alter and the changes that they have made. <u>Regardless of what is added on, the major feature of the contract should not be altered. Help from an estate lawyer is highly recommended.</u>

Adjustable rate mortgage (ARM): The interest rate on an adjustable mortgage usually changes frequently. For example, one may start with a mortgage with a low monthly payment in comparison to a fixed-rate mortgage. But because the interest rates fluctuate depending on the economy, the monthly payments on an ARM usually increase with time.

Adjustment date: The day your mortgage starts to accrue interest, even though you have not yet made a single mortgage payment, is known as the adjustment date. This adjustment date tends to fall on the <u>first day of the month </u>after the lender has advanced the mortgage funds.

Amortization refers to the schedule and duration of your mortgage payments that are spread over time. In real estate, a buyer's amortization schedule usually varies from 15-30 years.

Annual percentage rate (APR): When a mortgage is approved, the total amount of interest charged on the loan annually is referred to as the annual percentage rate.

Appraisal: Usually refers to an unbiased or independent estimate of the value of a home. When purchasing a home, the lender will usually require an independent third party to appraise the home to make sure that the amount of loan the buyer has requested is accurate. If the appraised value of the home is lower than what the buyer has offered, the lender may ask the buyer to make up the difference in the cost.

Appreciation: Reflects the amount the house value increases over time. To calculate the appreciation rate of a home, use the following formula:

Future home value = Present home value X (1 + interest rate)time in years

Assessed value: When an owner decides to sell a home, an assessment is usually done to determine how much tax he or she will owe on the property. The assessment is done by an assessor who calculates the value of the home by comparing the price with other similar homes in the same area and analyzing the home inspection report.

As-is: Sometimes, the seller will try to sell the property 'as is.' In most cases, the seller is not willing to do the repairs and simply wants to sell the home quickly. While the price of 'As is' homes can be low, one needs to have a great deal of experience purchasing such homes. Finally, 'as is' is the home condition at the time of the offer; if the property is not sold immediately, then the 'As is' condition may no longer be valid as, with time, something may have happened to the property.

Assignment: When a seller of a real estate property signs over the obligations and rights of a home to the buyer before the official closing, this is known as an assignment.

Assumable mortgage: Sometimes, the seller will transfer all the conditions and terms of his or her mortgage to the buyer- this is known as an assumable mortgage. Now the buyer simply takes over any residual debt belonging to the seller. This way, the buyer has no need to take out a new personal mortgage.

Backup offer: Sometimes, the buyer is interested in buying a property that the seller has agreed to a sale to someone else. In such a case, the buyer can submit a backup offer because sometimes the first offer may not fall through. Still, a backup offer has to be negotiated, and if a deposit is obtained, it must be documented. There can only be one backup offer.

Balloon mortgage: In general, most people obtain the conventional fixed-rate mortgage and repay the loan in monthly installments. On the other hand, a balloon mortgage is paid in one lump sum (balloon payment). These are short-term loans that are usually associated with construction projects or investments; they do not require any collateral. The downsides to balloon mortgages include 1) paying a large sum all at once 2) it is considered to be a high risk loan 3) can be difficult to finance and 4) can be difficult to find a lender for this type of loan.

Bi-weekly mortgage: Most people pay their mortgage on a monthly basis, but some homeowners have a biweekly mortgage payment plan. This means the owner makes two installments every month instead of one. At the end of each year, this will amount to <u>26 payments instead of 12</u>. People who can afford to make biweekly payments not only pay the principal balance faster but also save on interest rates.

Blind offer: Sometimes, a buyer may make an offer on a property that has not been seen. Such cases do occur when there is severe competition to buy homes. While risky, it does work.

Bridge loan: Sometimes, the owner will take out a short-term loan against his or her property to finance the purchase of another real estate property- this is known as a bridge loan. These loans are usually taken out for short periods that vary from a few weeks to several years.

Brokers: These are real estate professionals who have passed the licensing exam and acquired more education than what the state requires of real estate agents. Brokers have good knowledge of real estate law, property management, construction, and ethics. In most states, real estate agents are supervised by a broker.

Buydown: This is a mortgage financing deal that reduces the buyer's interest rates by a few years during the lifetime of a loan. In most cases, the contractor or the property seller will make payments to the mortgage lender; this will reduce the buyer's monthly payments and interest rates.

Call option: This is a legal contract that gives one party the right to sell and the other party the right to buy a piece of real estate sometime in the future at a defined price.

Cash-out refinance: Also referred to as cash-out-refi, is when a homeowner refinances the mortgage for more than its value and then withdraws the extra difference in cash. However, to meet the eligibility for this kind of loan, the borrower needs to have at <u>least 20% equity</u>.

Certificate of eligibility: When applying for a VA loan, the lender will ask the veteran for proof that he or she has met the minimum service requirements to qualify for a VA loan. The certificate of eligibility is needed for the application for a VA loan.

Certificate of reasonable value (CRV): This is a certificate issued by the Dept of Veterans Affairs. Any veteran who applies for a loan needs to have this certificate. The CRV helps establish the maximum value of the property so that the size of the loan can be determined.

Chain of titles: The chain of titles is similar to the blue book for residential homes. It documents the past owners of the property, starting with the very first owner.

Clear title: Also referred to as a 'good title' or 'free title', only reveals that there is no question of legal ownership of the property, including bad surveys or building code violations.

Closing: This is the end stage of a real estate deal. The date of closing is agreed upon when both the seller and buyer sign the contract. On the closing date, the property and title are then legally transferred to the buyer.

Closing costs: Usually account for <u>2% to 5%</u> of the total price of the home. They include fees charged by the lawyer, lender, insurance company, title company, HOA, real estate agent and other related companies. Based on Zillow surveys, the average home buyer in the US pays about $3,700 in closing costs; this fee is paid on the day of closing.

Co-borrower: Sometimes, the primary borrower may have difficulty obtaining a loan; in such cases, they can enlist the help of a co-borrower. This individual is usually a close friend or a family member who is added to the mortgage and guarantees the loan. The co-borrower is usually listed on the title and is able to sign loan documents. He or she is also under an obligation to pay the monthly payments if the primary buyer is unable to do so.

Commission: Real estate agents receive a commission of 5%-6% based on the home's sale price. This commission is usually divided between the seller and the buyer's agent; the money is paid at the time of the closing to the seller.

Common area assessments: When people reside in a home complex run by a homeowner association, some of the monthly fees go towards maintaining the common areas that are open to all the residents.

Comparable sales: Appraisers usually assess a home's value by comparing it to similar homes sold recently. Comparable sales comparisons are only valid for homes that have legally closed. Most insurance providers and lenders request that appraisers use at least three recent sales that have closed.

Construction loan: This is a short-term loan used to finance a real estate project or the construction of a home. This type of loan usually covers projected costs.

Contingency: When a contract or a property is contingent, certain things have to occur or transpire for the contract to remain valid. For example, a contingency may be that the home must pass an inspection first. Another example of contingency is that the seller may ask that the buyer sell their home within a specified date. If either party fails to meet the expected contingency, the contract may be voided.

Contingent vs. pending: When an owner has decided to accept an offer, the property is contingent as long as certain contractual exceptions are met. If all the contingencies are met, the property's status changes to 'pending.' A contingent offer can still be seen under active listings, whereas a pending offer will no longer be on the listings.

Covenants, conditions & restrictions (CC&Rs): These are rules and regulations on property that are run by the homeowner's association (HOA), a developer, or a neighborhood association. These rules and regulations limit what homeowners can do on their property. In addition, there are always monthly or annual fees associated with HOA.

Conventional mortgage: A loan that is usually not insured or guaranteed by the federal government. Borrowers of conventional mortgages tend to make large down payments and are not required to have mortgage insurance.

Conventional sale: In general, a conventional sale is when the property has no mortgage remaining, or the owner owes very little mortgage. Conventional sales are much easier to undertake compared to non-conventional sales like foreclosures, short sales, or prorated-related sales.

Convertible ARM: Convertible adjustable rate mortgages permit the buyer to take advantage of low-interest rates by obtaining a loan at a 'teaser' interest rate. While the monthly mortgage payments remain the same, the interest rates do fluctuate every six months. However, the borrower does have the choice of converting the ARM to a fixed-rate mortgage; but this switch also comes with fees.

Cost of funds index (COFI): This is the average of all the regional interest expenses acquired by the lender or financial institution. The COFI is then utilized to determine the variable rate loans.

Days-on-market (DOM): This refers to the duration of time the home has been actively listed for sale on the agent's multiple listing service. In general, if the home is on the listings for a short time and sold, the market usually favors sellers. If the home is on the listings for an indefinite time, the market is weak and usually favors buyers. Home selling and buying are seasonal, with most homes sold during spring. Winter months tend to have the slowest home sales.

Debt-to-income ratio (DTI): This is a number utilized by lenders and financial institutions to determine affordability by the buyer. The DTI ratio is obtained by tabulating the total debt expenses plus the monthly housing payment divided by the gross monthly income times 100. The DTI ratio helps lenders determine affordability by the buyer and gives them some idea of what the buyer may be able to afford on a monthly mortgage. Lenders prefer to have buyers who spend less than <u>28% of their total income on housing and less than 36% of their income on debt payments</u>. If either percentage is on the high side, the buyer will need to adjust the budget.

Deed: The home deed is a legally written document that transfers the title from the seller to the buyer. The deed also goes by another name: <u>'vehicle of the property interest transfer.'</u>

Deed-in-lieu of foreclosure: This is a document that transfers the property title from a homeowner to the lender/bank that holds the mortgage. A homeowner may submit a deed in lieu of foreclosure if the lender has denied them a loan modification or short sale. In most cases, the lenders/banks deny the request for a deed in lieu.

Default: Is said to occur when an owner defaults on the loan, meaning the loan agreed to in the contract is not paid. Default is said to occur when the homeowner has not made a loan payment in <u>90 days or more</u>.

Delinquency: Is said to occur when the owner has not made a scheduled payment. If the payment is delayed for more than <u>30 days</u>, the lender may initiate collections or even foreclosure proceedings.

Discount points: Also referred to as 'mortgage points,' these are fees that home buyers may sometimes pay to the bank/lender during closing. In return, the owner gets low-interest rates which can significantly reduce the monthly mortgage payments.

Down payment: This is the sum of money that a homebuyer pays at the time of closing. Typically most mortgages require a <u>20% down payment</u>. A conforming loan may accept a 5% downpayment, and an <u>FHA loan will accept a 3.5 % down payment.</u>

Due diligence: This is the time period available for the buyer to examine the property. For example, the buyer may want to hire an inspector before making an offer on the property. Sometimes the inspection may reveal a deficit, and then the buyer may want to renegotiate the contract or even terminate the contract, but this has to be done within a specified time period. Due diligence permits the buyer to fully understand and appreciate what he or she is purchasing.

Due-on-sale clause: Also known as an 'acceleration clause' it is a clause in the contract that protects lenders against below-market interest rates. This provision in the contract requires the seller of real estate to repay the full mortgage when the property is sold in the future.

Earnest money deposit: This is a small deposit that a homebuyer makes when entering into a contract with the seller. The deposit is 1%-5 % and shows that the buyer is genuinely interested in purchasing the property. The deposit is deducted from the closing and total down payment costs. This money is held in an escrow account.

Easement: Gives a person the legal right to use another individual's property or land while still retaining the title in the name of the owner.

Eminent domain: Permits the government the right to use or occupy a private property for public purposes. Eminent domain is only legal when the government adequately compensates the property owner for the land or property.

Encroachment: Is said to occur when a homeowner violates the neighbor's rights by adding or building on to a structure that extends into the neighbor's property line.

Encumbrance: In real estate, it refers to any claim against a real estate property that limits its transfer or use, including an easement or property tax lien.

Equal Credit Opportunity Act (ECOA) was enacted in 1974. The law made it unlawful for lenders and creditors to discriminate against applicants based on color, race, religion, sex, marital status, national origin, or age just because they were recipients of public assistance.

Equity: This is the property that you actually own outright. When you have a mortgage, your mortgage lender also has an interest in your property until you have fully paid off the loan. To calculate the home equity, subtract the residual mortgage balance from the current market value of your home. Home equity generally increases as you pay off your loan or the market value of your property increases. For example, if you purchase a property worth $300,000 for $275,000, you gain what is known as instant equity of $25,000. When you sell the property you bought for $275,000 for $290,000, you'll get to keep the equity in the home after the closing once all the expenses are paid.

Escrow: This is a feature of the home-buying process. It usually involves a third party that will hold on to the funds during the transaction. When the transaction is complete, the third party will release the funds to the seller.

Examination of title: Allows one to review all the public records linked to the property. The review will look at the Wills, past deeds, and trusts to ensure that the title has passed legally and cleanly to the new owner.

Exclusive listing: This is a tactic sometimes utilized to encourage the agent to sell the property fast- usually within a specified time (e.g., months). If the agent can sell the property fast, he will gain the commission irrespective how the buyer was discovered or solicited.

Fair Credit Reporting Act (FCRA): The act was passed in 1970 to ensure accuracy, fairness, and privacy of personal data contained in the data bank by the credit reporting agencies. The key reason for this act was to protect home buyers from having their personal and financial information used against them.

Fair market value: Refers to the property's value in an open and free market under the condition that the seller and buyer are aware of the value.

Fee simple: Reflects the most common type of property ownership. In simple terms, it means that the owner has indefinite rights to the property; and that the rights may be inherited or transferred when the owner wants. The fee simple is most frequently associated with condominiums, single-family homes, and townhomes that are purchased under some conditions, covenants, and restrictions.

FHA mortgage: The federal housing administration loans have been around for at least 90 years and were introduced to assist first-time homebuyers. The FHA not only insures the loans but offers several benefits, including a low down payment (which may be <u>as low as 3.5% of the total home value</u>), easy credit qualifying, and low closing costs. Lenders feel confident about giving FHA loans because they are insured by a governmental agency.

Fixed-rate mortgage: This is a common type of loan that comes with a fixed interest rate that will last for the lifetime of the loan. It provides the borrower with predictability and stability over the lifetime of the loan. Consumers prefer a fixed-rate mortgage because it is reliable, but of course, you need to make sure that the interest rates are low.

For sale by owner: A relatively new trend that is fast catching on is for sale by the owner. These homes are sold without any assistance from a real estate agent. A key benefit to the seller is that he or she avoids paying commission fees.

Foreclosure: When the homeowner is unable or does not make the regular monthly mortgage payments, usually for more than <u>three months</u>, the property can be foreclosed. This legal process will ensure that the owner no longer has any property rights. If the owner is no longer able to pay the outstanding debt on the property or sell the home via a short sale, the property then enters a foreclosure auction. If the home still cannot be sold, the lender will take control of the property.

Hard money loan: Some people with bad credit may not be able to get financing from banks or private lenders. Thus, they resort to hard money loans that are financially based on the property and not the credit score. Usually, these loans require a large down payment, have high-interest rates, and have a short repayment schedule. These loans are often small.

Home Equity Conversion Mortgage (HECM): This is an <u>FHA reverse mortgage</u> program that assists homeowners in withdrawing equity on their home via a line of credit, a fixed monthly payment, or a combination of the two.

Home equity line of credit (HELOC): This program provides owners with a revolving credit line that can be used to pay for large expenses or consolidate high-interest debt loans like credit cards.

Home inspection: This is now a routine event done prior to the purchase of a home. The inspection is done by an independent third party that verifies the status and condition of the property. The inspector will report on things like the home's structure, foundation, roof, heating system, etc. If major issues are identified in the home, it can affect the value and sale of the home. The buyer may opt not to buy the home until the deficits are fixed.

Homeowner's association (HOA): This is an entity that regulates townhomes, condominiums, and many other developmental properties. Anyone who purchases a property in such a complex has to join the HOA and pay the monthly or annual fees. The people running the HOA are members of the housing community and set the rules and regulations. The HOA fees cover repairs, maintenance, and upkeep of the property. The more services offered by the building complex, the higher the HOA fees. Homeowners who fail to comply with the rules or fail to pay the maintenance fees may have a lien placed on the property or even have the home foreclosed.

Homeowner's insurance: Anyone who purchases a home in America must have homeowners insurance to cover any damages or losses that may occur following a natural disaster, theft, or accident. The homeowner's insurance may also protect the owner from liability from any type of accident both inside and outside the home. In most cases, the insurance payments are included as part of the monthly mortgage payments.

iBuyer: This is a recent novel introduction to the world of real estate. These companies use technology to make an offer on a home instantly. iBuyers also helps with marketing, opening, and reselling your home. Depending on the type of service selected, the big benefit is that you have more control over when you move, and it saves you time.

Inspection: Prior to finalizing a home purchase, most potential buyers will order an independent third-party home inspection. The reason for the inspection is to check the condition of the home and determine if any major repairs are necessary. Once the report is available, the buyer can ask the seller to make the necessary repairs or reduce the selling price of the home.

Inspection contingency: Also referred to as 'due diligence contingency' the inspection clause is usually inserted into the purchase agreement. This agreement grants the potential home buyer a specified amount of time during escrow to perform a home inspection.

Judicial foreclosure: This is a mandatory legal process in some states. It requires that all foreclosed homes first go through the legal system to confirm that the owner has defaulted before the home can be placed for auction. The ultimate aim of judicial foreclosure is to protect property owners from unethical and corrupt lenders.

Jumbo loan: This is a mortgage for an amount that greatly exceeds the cap limit set by government-sponsored agencies like Fannie Mae and Freddie Mac. Hence if you are purchasing a home or a mansion in a wealthy neighborhood like Great Neck or Silicon Valley, you may need a jumbo loan. However, the eligibility criteria for jumbo loans are very strict, and the loan itself is manually underwritten to reduce the risk to the lender.

Land lease: In most cases, when a home is purchased, the buyer owns the house and the land the property was built on. However, there are occasions when a land lease may be involved, which means that the home belongs to the owner, but they will have to pay rent to the landowner of the land.

Lease option: This feature offers people who rent an option to own real estate. This option provides the lessee the ability to rent (lease) the property with an option to purchase. The contract will detail the monthly rental with an option to buy at any time during the length of the residence. The purchase price of the home is usually determined at the time of the lease signing process.

Lender: In the world of real estate, the lender often refers to a financial institution, an individual, or a private company that lends money to the buyer to purchase real estate. In every case, the lender will set forth a contract and set details on when the loan is to be paid back and the total interest.

Lien: When there is an unpaid debt on a piece of real estate, the lender may place a lien on the property. This is a legal notice that states the bank/lender will undertake legal steps to recover the money owed/debt. The lien may be placed as a result of unpaid property tax, a court judgment, or unpaid bills. A lien can prevent the owner from selling the property until the debt is resolved.

Life cap: When a buyer obtains a mortgage on an adjustable rate, there is a cap on the maximum amount of interest rate over the lifetime of the loan- this is known as a life cap. It is also referred to as the 'interest rate ceiling' or 'absolute interest rate.' The life cap helps prevent unreasonable ballooning of the interest rate on loans.

Loan contingency: Also referred to as a 'mortgage contingency,' it is an addendum or a clause in the contract that permits the potential buyer to back out of the deal and get the deposit back in case he or she is not able to secure a mortgage. There is usually a time period for the loan contingency clause to be valid.

Loan officer: Also known as 'mortgage loan officer' or 'residential loan officer,' these professionals help homebuyers with the refinancing or purchase of a home. Loan officers are usually employed by lending institutions and assist potential home buyers in selecting the right type of loan. They also help communicate with appraisers and assist with the loan application.

Loan origination: This is defined as the process when a potential home buyer submits an application for a loan from a private lender or financial institution. The loan origination fee charged for processing the loan varies from 0.5% to 1% of the total loan amount.

Loan servicing: This is terminology to describe the administrative aspects of maintaining the loan from the time the loan was given to the time when it is fully paid. The loan servicing program includes keeping records of all payments and balances, sending the monthly borrower statements, and paying taxes and insurance. The loan servicing is usually performed by the loan lender.

Loan-to-value ratio (LTV): The LTV ratio is the loan balance on the mortgage divided by the value of the home. It reflects how much the owner has borrowed from a lender as a percentage of the appraised value of the home. The higher the LTV ratio, the greater the risk during loan underwriting because it reflects a low down payment, low equity, or lack of ownership of the property. It is usually associated with a high risk of loan default.

Lock-in period: This is the time period during which the borrower is unable to repay the loan in full without facing a monetary penalty by the lender.

Mortgage: This is a financial agreement between a lender and a borrower where the former gets the rights to the borrower's property. If the borrower fails or is unable to make the monthly payments upon an agreed time, the lender has the legal right to seize the property.

Mortgage banker: This is an individual who works for a financial institution or a private lender to provide funds to a borrower. The mortgage banker is only able to obtain funds from a specific institution and is also responsible for the mortgage process, including overseeing the application, evaluating the property, and performing a credit check on the borrower.

Mortgage broker: This is an individual who often acts as a middleman between the borrower and the lending institutions. The broker compares mortgages from different lenders and tries to give the borrower the best deal in town.

Mortgage insurance: When a homebuyer purchases a home with less than 20% of the down payment or is the recipient of a USDA or FHA loan, the individual will have to purchase mortgage insurance. While this can increase the cost of the loan, it lowers the risks to the lender.

Mortgage pre-approval letter: When applying for a loan, it is important to get a preapproval letter from the lender. This letter usually reveals the type of loan, the terms, and the loan amount the buyer has qualified for. Prior to getting the preapproval letter, the lender will check the buyer's credit history, cash on hand, and the debt to income ratio. Obtaining a mortgage pre-approval letter is helpful as it gives the homebuyer some idea of what he or she can afford. Plus, it reassures the seller that the buyer does have the finances available to purchase a home.

Multiple Listing Service (MLS): This is a comprehensive collection of at least 700 regional databases, each with its own listings. Each database has its own local listings. It permits brokers and realtors to access and add information on real estate properties for sale in a particular area. The buyer's agent will frequently check MLS to determine what property is on the market and the price of similar homes. Agents have to pay dues to access the MLS database.

Natural hazards disclosure (NHD): The NHD is a state-required report that discloses if the property is located in a location where there is a higher risk of natural hazards or disasters. There is a fee associated with the report that is paid by the seller and given to the buyer. Common natural hazards covered in the report include:

• Areas prone to flooding

• Areas with high fire hazard

• Wildland areas that have a high forest fire risk

• Zone of earthquake

Negative amortization: Amortization is the process of paying off the loan with regular payments so that each month the amount of the loan decreases. <u>Negative amortization occurs when you pay less than the scheduled monthly payments</u>, and the amount you owe tends to increase.

No cash-out refinance: This is a type of loan sometimes used by the borrower to improve the rate on the loan. To be of benefit, it should shorten the lifespan of the loan. With no cash refinancing, the borrower refinances an existing loan for equal to or less than the outstanding loan balance. The idea behind it is to reduce the interest rates on the loan.

No-cost mortgage: This is a type of refinancing where the lender pays the loan settlement costs for the borrower. In exchange, the borrower will have a loan with higher interest rates. In turn, the mortgage lender will sell the loan to a secondary mortgage market for a much higher price due to the high-interest rate.

Note rate: This is the interest rate documented on the mortgage document. It is also referred to as the 'face interest rate' or 'nominal rate.'

Offer/counter offer: Potential home buyers usually make an initial offer on the property they want to purchase. This offer may be based on what the agent deems to be fair market value or may be lower. The offer is usually made in writing and submitted to the seller by the agent. The seller may accept the offer or may make a counteroffer. The two parties often negotiate until they come to a price that is mutually agreeable.

Original principal balance: This is the amount the buyer owes on the mortgage before even making the very first payment.

Origination fee: The <u>cost of processing the loan application</u> is called the origination fee.

Owner financing: Also referred to as 'seller financing,' this occurs when the potential buyer finances the home purchase through the seller, thus bypassing the usual financial institutions and private lenders.

Pending: A real estate sale is said to be pending when the buyer and seller have met all the contingencies and are moving towards closing. At this stage, the sale of the home is most likely; otherwise, the seller or buyer is at risk of losing money if they walk out on the deal.

Per Diem: These are fees that are charged by the day if the loan completion is not approved on the scheduled day. On closing, the lender will demand this payment.

PITI: In short, this abbreviation reflects the principle, interest, taxes, and insurance. It usually refers to the total sum of these charges that are quoted every month. PITI costs are calculated and compared to the borrower's monthly gross income prior to approving a loan. In general, the borrower's PITI costs should be less than <u>28% of their gross monthly income</u>.

Planned unit development (PUD): This is a housing complex made up of townhomes, single-family residences, condominiums -- as well as commercial units. PUDs may offer some common areas and amenities (e.g., tennis courts, playgrounds, etc.) that are owned by the HOA.

Pre-approval: Before making an offer on a home, the buyer should get a preapproval letter from the lender. The lender will usually do a credit check, verify all the information, do the debt-to-income ratio and approve the buyer for a specified amount of <u>loan for up to 90 days</u>. The pre-approval letter will indicate the amount of the downpayment plus the interest rate on the loan. A preapproval letter is more complete than a pre-qualification letter.

Pre-qualification: This is slightly different from pre-approval; it just gives a rough estimate of how much the potential buyer can afford to buy a home. Getting pre-qualified is a simple matter based solely on what the buyer tells the lender; it <u>is not based on verified information or proof</u>.

Preliminary report: This report gives insight into any problems with the home title. Any title issues need to be worked out with the seller before purchase. The preliminary report will provide details on past ownership, easements, and liens. In most cases, this data can be obtained from the local county recorder's office. The preliminary report is necessary for the insurance company before it can issue a title insurance policy. The majority of lenders recommend that borrowers purchase title insurance coverage to protect their assets. Sometimes the seller will pay for the policy.

Prime interest rate: This is generally a favored interest rate that is given to the lender's loyal and reliable customers. It is usually the best available loan rate that is usually three points above the federal fund rate, the rate which banks charge each other for overnight loans.

Principal: This is the actual amount of money owed on the loan without any interest. As one starts to make the monthly mortgage payment, the principal starts to go down. However, with most loans, one first pays off the interest rate. If the amount of interest on the loan is high, you, in fact, pay less on the principal. In such cases, the borrower will usually end up paying much more for the mortgage with time.

Probate sale: When a homeowner dies suddenly without a will or without leaving the home to someone, then the property goes to probate, which is a legal process. The probate court then decides who will receive the property. Probate is an expensive process and time-consuming. A probate sale is complex and may take many months, even if the case is simple, but if there are multiple people claiming ownership, probate can take years to resolve.

Proof of funds: When a potential buyer makes an offer, the seller will often ask for proof of funds. If you are purchasing a home with a mortgage, then the bank will provide you with a pre-approval letter. If you are paying cash for the home, you will have to show the seller that you actually have the money. Documents that qualify as proof of funds include:

1. Online bank statement or original letter from a bank

2. Certified financial statements that show cash flow or income.

3. Copy of a money market account on a letterhead

4. An open equity line of credit

Purchase and sale agreement: This is essentially a contract between the seller and buyer that outlines the terms of the parties to purchase and sell real estate property. When a purchase and sell agreement has been signed, it usually reveals that the seller and buyer have formalized their commitment to purchase and sell the real estate property.

Purchase agreement: This agreement reveals that the buyer is interested in buying a piece of property that is up for sale. The purchase agreement will outline the terms and conditions of the sale. It is a legal document that holds both parties accountable for meeting their obligations.

Purchase-money mortgage: Also referred to as seller or owner refinancing, it is issued to the buyer by the home seller during the transaction. This venture is done to bypass the usual mortgage broker or lender and permits the buyer to assume the seller's remaining mortgage.

Quitclaim deed: This is a document that transfers ownership of the home/property from one person to another individual. Even though it transfers the title of the property but in reality only transfers only what the seller owns. For example, if two individuals jointly own a home, one individual can only transfer his or her half of the property via the quit claim deed. This type of transaction is often utilized when the property is being transferred among family members who do not use the established real estate pathway.

Rate lock: This is a process that permits borrowers to lock into low or advantageous interest rates before the real estate deal is closed. The rate lock permits the borrower to remain with that specific interest rate for a specific amount of time.

Real estate agent: A professional who is licensed to coordinate and negotiate the selling and buying of real estate. The majority of real estate agents work for brokers or realtors who have additional experience, certification, and training.

Real estate owned: This refers to real estate that is owned by a governmental agency, bank, or private lender. The homes usually become REO following an unsuccessful short sale or foreclosure auction. There are some buyers who thrive on REO properties because every now and then they find a great home sold cheaply that requires minimal repairs. Frequently the lender or the bank will market the property for sale 'As is'- meaning they are not willing to make any property repairs; for the buyer, this can prove to be a burst or a boom.

Real Estate Settlement Procedures Act (RESPA): This law requires lenders to provide <u>disclosures to borrowers</u> of all real estate transactions, consumer protection laws, and settlement services. The key goals of RESPA are to regulate the costs of settlement, limit the use of escrow accounts, and ban practices that involve kickbacks.

Realtor: This is another term for a licensed real estate agent. However, not all realtors are licensed. Realtors usually join the National Association of Realtors (NAR). Realtors maintain a high standard of practice and promise to be ethical in their dealings with each other and the clients they serve.

Refinance: This is a refinancing transaction that involves the replacement of the existing loan with a new loan. However, when a borrower refinances, the debt is not eliminated. Refinancing, however, tends to offer better loan terms, including lower monthly mortgage payments, reduced interest rates, or a shorter loan term. But there is a fee associated with refinancing.

Rent-back: Also known as 'leaseback,' it is a deal/arrangement between the new home buyer and seller. Under the agreement, the buyer permits the seller (now tenant) to reside in the home even after the close of escrow. The agreement terms are always worked out ahead of time and usually involve a daily rental fee, lease deposit, and the duration of time the seller can remain in the home. The fee charged to the seller may include the new homeowner's monthly mortgage as well as a fee for any inconvenience that has caused the delay for a move-in.

Right of ingress or egress: The right of <u>ingress</u> means that the person has the right to enter a property, and the right to <u>egress</u> means that the person has the legal right to exit the property. These terms are usually used in an easement or rental scenario where a tenant or an individual has been granted access to a private road, shared driveway, etc.

Right of survivorship: This is a process used when there is joint ownership of tenancy or a property. It ensures that the surviving owner will automatically receive the deceased owner's share of the property and will now become the sole property owner.

Sale-leaseback: This occurs when the buyer closes on a property and then decides to lease the tenancy back to the seller. This situation occurs <u>when the seller is unable to move out of the property after the closing date</u>. In this case, the buyer becomes a temporary landlord and will charge the seller a rental fee for every day he or she remains in the home.

Second mortgage: This is a loan that a property owner borrows against the value of the home. Also referred to as HELOCs, the loan draws on the market value of the home and provides the borrower with a line of credit or lump sum. The loan is then paid back in regular payments.

Secured loan: This is a loan that is backed by assets belonging to the borrower. This may include cars, jewelry, or other large items that can be used as a payment to the bank/lender when the borrower is unable or fails to repay the loan.

Seller carry-back: This is a financial transaction where the seller acts as a financial institution or bank for some or all the transactions. The seller will usually ask the buyer to sign a promissory note acknowledging the transaction and agreeing to pay a set amount of money to the seller. Once the deal is signed, the seller will transfer the title to the new owner. If the buyer fails to make the monthly payments, the seller is legally allowed to foreclose and take back the property.

Seller concession: Sometimes, sellers may sweeten the deal for the potential buyers by offering a range of concessions. They may include paying for the buyer's closing costs, the cost of a home inspection, etc. This endeavor leaves more money in the buyer's pocket. It works well when homes are hard to sell.

Seller's disclosure: This concerns the transparency of the home information by the seller. If the seller does not disclose all the facts about the home, the buyer may elect not to purchase the home. The seller is required by law to disclose all the information to the best of his or her knowledge. Besides disclosing problems inside the home, the seller must also be truthful about any problems outside the home like property disputes with the neighbor, pest issues, any potential reconstruction near the home in the future, noise level, running trains, unusual odor from nearby commercial establishments, etc.

Servicer: This is an individual who services mortgages. He or she performs the administrative paperwork associated with a loan, responds to borrower inquiries, processes loan payments, and tracks all payments, including the interest.

Short sale: in general, with a short sale, the property in question is being sold for much less than the debt secured by the property. However, short sales do need the approval of the lender because the proceeds of the sale will be 'short' of the amount owed. Because lenders do not want to lose money, the process of approving a short sale is a long and drawn-out affair, often requiring more time to close than a conventional home sale.

Subject to inspection: This means that the seller has set a condition; the property cannot be viewed without an accepted offer. Some of the reasons for this notice include 1) uncooperative tenants and 2) privacy concerns of the residing occupants. For most conventional home buyers, the idea of purchasing a property unseen may seem frightening, but for the savvy investor, this strategy can be used to lower the asking price. Finally, one has to remember that under the standard purchasing contract, the buyer still has the option to inspect the home within a certain time period; and one can always cancel the sale agreement without a penalty during this period.

Tenancy in common (TIC): This is a term to describe a type of joint ownership of a property, whether it is a commercial building or a single-family residence. While the common tenants own the property, the ratio of ownership may be different. Funding for such a property depends on the type of property and can be difficult. Also of relevance is that the tenants in common do not automatically have the right to survivorship, meaning that the surviving owners cannot just split up the deceased tenant's property among them. Instead, the deceased tenant's ownership interest/percentage will be distributed according to the will or probate.

Termite report: Termites can be a problem in some homes, and these insects can cause havoc on the property by feeding and destroying the wood. Potential home buyers should get a termite report which will reveal the extent of the termite problem and the degree of damage. The termite report will also include a diagram of the property with the location of termites. The report will also offer solutions such as tenting or spraying to get rid of the termites. The cost of getting rid of termites is not usually stated in the report.

Title search: This is a process that allows anyone to examine the public records for the home history, including prior sales, purchases, outstanding tax, and liens. A title search allows one to find out the real property owner. Any tax issues or liens against the property are also listed in the records. One can do a title search online or visit the local county office.

Title: Refers to the rights of the property. The rights to a property are usually transferred from the seller to the buyer during the sale of the home. At closing, the buyer is given the title and legal rights to the home.

Transfer of ownership: In real estate, a transfer of ownership is said to have occurred when the seller provides the title and property deed to the buyer at closing.

Transfer tax: This is a transaction fee for the transfer of a property's title. The transfer tax is imposed by the local county and state where the transaction takes place. The fee is based on the property's classification and value. In most cases, the seller will pay the real estate transfer tax unless it is stated otherwise in the contract.

Trust sale: This usually means that the property is being sold by a trustee named in the living trust. In most cases, the trustee becomes the seller because the primary homeowner has passed away, is disabled, or has placed the assets in a living trust to be managed by a trustee. The downside of using a trustee is that this individual or agency may not spend a great deal of time looking for the best buyer or may not care who buys the property because of a lack of sentimental value. Worse, the trustee may sell the home for much less than its real value. Some trustees may simply want to offload the property and move on with life.

Under contract: When a seller accepts an offer from a buyer, either verbal or written, this usually means that there is a contract, even though no formal transaction has taken place.

VA mortgage: The VA has a financial program that helps veterans, service members, and eligible surviving spouses to receive home loan guarantees provided by private lenders. The VA loans have very favorable terms for the borrower. The VA loans require very little or no down payment, offer competitive interest rates and low administrative fees.

Chapter 2: Home Equity Conversion Mortgage (HECM)

1. The home equity conversion mortgage (HECM) is a <u>type of reverse mortgage</u> that is fully insured by the FHA. The HECM allows seniors to convert the equity in their homes into cash.

2. The total amount of loan that a senior can borrow depends on the appraised value of the home.

3. In addition, the borrower must be at least <u>62 years old</u>.

4. After the loan is made, interest accrues, but the borrower makes no payments until the home is sold, moves out of the property, or dies- at this time, the entire loan needs to be repaid.

5. HECMs make up most reverse mortgages on the real estate market; while much more favorable than proprietary reverse mortgages, HECMs have a cap on the maximum amount of loan.

6. Plus, <u>all borrowers need PMI</u>.

HECMs usually come with low-interest rates, but a lot depends on the age of the borrower and how long the borrower expects to own or reside in the home. In most cases, the repayment is only made after the borrower dies or sells the home.

A HECM is similar in several respects to a home equity loan since borrowers accept cash advances based on the equity of the home. However, with a home equity loan, the borrower usually repays the money in monthly payments after the loan is given.

Loan Sponsorship

The home equity conversion mortgage is <u>sponsored by the FHA</u>, which sets eligibility criteria and limits on the loans. Borrowers can only obtain HECMs from financial institutions where FHA sponsors the financial products. To qualify for a HECM, the borrower must first complete an application form and meet the following requirements:

• Be the owner of the property or have paid a significant amount of money toward the property

• Be at least 62 years old

• Not have any federal debt

• The property is the primary residence

• Engage in an interactive consumer information session with a counselor provided by the Housing and Urban Development

• Be able to make regular payments on insurance, property taxes, HOA fees, etc

In addition, there are also residential property requirements that include the following:

• The residence has to be a single-family home or it can be a two- to four-unit home. The borrower must be a resident in one of the units for eligibility since this is not an investment loan.

• An FHA or HUD-approved condominium

• A manufactured home that meets FHA requirements

Making a Complaint

Consumers who feel they have been discriminated against in obtaining a mortgage based on religion, race, marital status, sex, national origin, disability, or use of public assistance can file a report with the Consumer Financial Protection Bureau or with HUD.

Differences Between a HECM and a Reverse Mortgage

1. All HECMs are considered to be reverse mortgages, but on the other hand, not all traditional reverse loans are home equity conversion mortgages.

2. The HECM is insured by the FHA but it is only issued by a lender approved by the FHA.

3. The fact is consumers should know that with a HECM reverse mortgage, it is possible to lose the home. If the owner fails to maintain the property, not pay property taxes or insurance, the home can be seized. If the property is no longer the primary residence for more than 12 consecutive months or even if the individual is admitted to a nursing home, hospital, or long-term facility, he or she can lose the home if the balance on the reverse mortgage is not paid.

Is a HECM Loan Expensive?

Even though HECM loans do not require monthly payments, they do have fees for servicing and closing; plus, the borrower has to buy PMI. These fees can be rolled into the loan.

Good Alternative to a HECM

Downsize the home, and one may not need the extra income

The Bottom Line

The HECM is the most common type of reverse mortgage. It permits senior homeowners to tap into their home equity without having to pay it back until they die or move away from home.

Chapter 3: SAFE Act

Secure and Fair Enforcement of Mortgages Act (SAFE ACT): (Regulation G).

1. The Secure and Fair Enforcement for Mortgage Licensing Act of 2008 (SAFE Act) was enacted right after the <u>2008 housing crisis</u>.

2. The Act mandated a nationwide registration and licensing system for residential mortgage loan originators (MLOs).

3. The <u>SAFE Act prohibits individuals from conducting any type of transaction that deals with residential mortgages/loans without first registering and maintaining the license.</u>

4. For individuals who are employees of a covered financial agency, one needs to have a federally issued unique identifier and be registered as a registered mortgage loan originator.

5. All other people need to register and have a state license to function as a licensed mortgage loan originator. In addition, these individuals must also have a state issued unique identifier, that is available at registration.

6. The SAFE Act mandates that state licensing and federal registration can be completed via the online registration system, the Nationwide Mortgage Licensing System and Registry.

The aim of the SAFE Act include the following:

1. Improving and aggregating information flow to and between regulators

2. Ensuring that there is greater accountability and tracking of MLOs

3. Enhance consumer protections

4. Boost anti-fraud measures

5. Provide borrowers and potential home buyers with all the necessary information at no cost regarding the conduct, employment history, and all past enforcement actions/disciplinary measures against mortgage loan officers.

Chapter 4: USDA Loans

1. The USDA loan is a government-sponsored loan that requires <u>no down payment</u>; it comes with low-interest rates comparable to other government-backed programs like the VA and FHA.

2. The one criterion for loan eligibility is that the <u>home must be in a rural</u> or less densely populated area, like farmland or the outskirts of the city.

3. It is estimated that 91% of the land in the US is considered rural, and for those buyers wanting a home in a less populated area, a USDA loan may be the right way to go.

4. USDA loans are great home loans for first-time buyers.

Brief History of USDA Loans

1. The USDA loan's origins go back to 1949 with the passing of the <u>American Housing Act.</u>

2. After the Second World War ended, it was evident that US housing was in short

supply, and millions of families were sharing or renting homes. Homeownership was rare in those days chiefly because getting a loan was difficult, and the interest rates were in the double digits.

3. Meanwhile, economic studies showed that homeownership could help build and strengthen weakened US communities and create jobs that could lead to greater tax revenue and boost the GDP. With this in mind, the American Housing Act was born.

4. This law allowed millions of Americans to buy homes instead of being perpetual renters. Many new mortgage loans were made available, and one of them was the USDA mortgage.

How Do USDA Loans Work?

The USDA loan is guaranteed by the US Dept of Agriculture, which tells the lender that there is a low risk of not being paid back; in return, lenders would offer low-interest rates with no down payment.

In general, a credit score of 640 is required for a USDA loan, but borrowers with lower scores are also eligible if they have a solid job history.

Types of USDA Loans

Only two types of USDA mortgages are available:

1) the 15-year fixed-rate loans and

2) 30-year fixed-rate loans.

The USDA does not offer adjustable-rate mortgages (ARMs)

Qualifying for a USDA Loan

• Be a legal US resident

• Have a dependable source of income

• Prove creditworthiness

• Be a resident in the rural area

• Have a household income that <u>equals 115% or slightly lower</u> than the median income of the local area.

USDA Vs. FDA Loans

1. Unlike the USDA loan, FHA loans require the borrower to make a 3.5% down payment<u>- with USDA; there is no need for any down payment</u>.

2. FHA loans require a credit score of 500, whereas <u>USDA loans enforce a minimum score of 580.</u>

3. FHA loans can be used for any 1-4 unit home; <u>USDA loans are limited to 1 unit home.</u>

4. With an FHA loan, <u>there are no strict location requirements.</u>

5. Unlike FHA and other government-backed mortgages, there is no cap on the maximum amount of loan available with the USDA mortgage program.

The USDA Loan

USDA loans are best for people who prefer to purchase a home in a less densely populated area of the country. These loans are also easy to refinance as long as you have paid your mortgage promptly over the past 12 months.

A USDA loan will also provide a loan for home repair and improvements like roof remodeling, accessibility for a disabled person, or making the home energy efficient.

USDA mortgages are portable (Assumable), meaning that the loan can be transferred to future buyers of the property at the same interest rate.

Chapter 5: Homeowners Protection Act

1. The Homeowners Protection Act is a federal law that was <u>enacted in 1998</u>.

2. The key aim of this law was to ensure that <u>borrowers would not pay unnecessary mortgage insurance,</u> if it was not required. For example, if the borrower has already reached a mortgage principal of 20%, PMI is no longer needed.

3. The Homeowners Protection Act covers all residential and private mortgages purchased after 1999.

4. The Homeowners Protection Act, also referred to as the PMI Cancellation Act makes it mandatory for banks and lenders to disclose specific information related to PMI.

5. The law also recommends that the PMI be automatically canceled for a borrower who has accumulated the required home equity and thus does not need to purchase or pay PMI.

6. Prior to the Act, many homeowners had great difficulty canceling the PMI.

7. <u>The homeowner's protection act doesn't apply to FHA and VA loans.</u>

PMI is generally canceled once the borrower pays off at least 20% of the mortgage principal or when the loan-to-value ratio reaches 80. However, many unscrupulous lenders in the past used to continue with PMI indefinitely, and worse, cancellation of the PMI was difficult in the past.

With the Homeowners Protection Act, lenders are not allowed lifelong PMI on loans and must cancel the PMI once the owner reaches a home equity of 20%. Compliance with the Homeowners Protection Act is monitored and enforced by the CFPB.

Chapter 6: The Federal Housing Administration (FHA) Loan

1. The Federal Housing Administration <u>offers a home loan that is insured by the government but issued by both a private lender</u> and a bank that has been approved by the agency.

2. Compared to other loans, FHA loans only <u>require a low down payment</u>.

3. In addition, borrowers tend to have lower credit scores than what is required for conventional loans.

4. FHA loans are designed to assist low to moderate-income families in purchasing a home. Many of these borrowers may have been rejected by other lenders.

5. Overall, borrowers of <u>FHA loans are considered high risk and consequently have to pay high-interest rates and also obtain private mortgage insurance</u>.

6. However, since the loans are insured by the government, lenders are willing to provide the loan even though the credit scores may be low and the small down payment.

7. Remember, the FHA does not loan any money- the money is loaned by lenders and banks. The FHA just guarantees the loan.

The FHA was created in 1934 when the housing industry was in a mess with skyrocketing foreclosures, and a downpayment of 50% was required to get a loan. Prior to the 2nd World War, most Americans did not own a home.

Thus, the FHA was created to make home buying easy and lower the risk for lenders; by 2000, homeownership in the USA was close to 70%.

How Does an FHA Loan Work?

1. Even with a credit score of 600 or less, the borrower can obtain 96.5% of the home value of the loan. The minimum downpayment required is only 3.5%

2. If the credit score is between 500-579, an FHA loan is possible, but it requires a bigger down payment of at least 10%.

3. Everyone is eligible for FHA loans, including those who are eligible for conventional loans. But overall, borrowers with strong finances and good credit may be better off with a conventional loan since they will not need to purchase insurance.

Subtypes of FHA Loans

Besides the traditional loans, The FHA also has at least half a dozen home loans that include the following:

1. The Home Equity Conversion Mortgage (HECM) is a <u>reverse mortgage program</u> for people over the age of 62. The loan helps convert the equity in the home to cash, so the owner still retains the title.

2. FHA 203(k) Improvement Loan is for repairs and renovations and repairs.

3. FHA Energy Efficient Mortgage is like the FHA 203k loan but is focused on upgrades that will lower utility bills, like installing solar systems and insulating the home

4. The Section 245 Loan is meant for individuals who expect their incomes to increase in the near future. The Graduated Payment Mortgage (GPM) usually begins with low monthly payments but over time, these payments will increase. The Growing-Equity Mortgage (GEM) is a loan that comes with pre-arranged increases in the monthly principal payments. Both these loans are of short duration.

What are FHA Loan Requirements?

• Valid social security number

• State of residence

• Legal age

• Work history over the past two years

• Ability to pay bills

Denials for FHA Loans

1. Those who fall behind with <u>their federal student loan payments or income tax are usually rejected.</u>

2. A history of foreclosure is also a reason for denial. <u>At least 2-3 years</u> must have passed

since the borrower filed for bankruptcy to be eligible.

3. To qualify for an FHA loan, the mortgage payment, property taxes, HOA fees, homeowners insurance, and mortgage insurance <u>should not be more than 31% of gross income (also known as the FRONT END RATIO).</u>

4. At the same time, <u>the back-end ratio</u>, which includes the mortgage payment and all the other monthly living expenses, should not be more than <u>43% of the gross income</u>.

FHA Mortgage Insurance Premiums (MIPs)

1. For the borrower of an FHA loan, there are two subtypes of mortgage insurance premiums (MIPs): one is the upfront MIP and the second is the yearly MIP, which is paid every month.

2. In 2022, <u>the upfront MIP equaled 1.75%</u> of the price of the home loan.

3. The borrower does have a choice of paying the MIP; the upfront MIP can be paid at the time of closing or the MIP can be combined with the loan; and one single payment is required for both.

4. For example, if you have obtained a home loan for $450,000, the upfront MIP will be 1.75% x $450,000 = $7,875.

5. These insurance payments are deposited into an escrow account that is managed by the U.S. Treasury.

6. If the borrower defaults on the loan, the money being held in the escrow account will be used to repay the residual mortgage.

7. The MIP payments may vary from 0.4% to 1.05% of the price of the home loan. The payment amounts are variable and depend on the length of the loan, amount of loan and the initial loan-to-value ratio; the higher the loan to value ratio -the bigger the

payments.

8. The insurance payments and premiums do offer a tax deduction.

Homes That Qualify for an FHA Loan

1. To obtain an FHA loan, the property financed must be owner-occupied and be the principal residence. What this means is that an FHA loan is not intended for renewal or investment properties.

2. Homes that are eligible for FHA financing include semi-detached and detached homes, row homes, townhouses, and condos that have been FHA-approved.

3. Further, the property must be appraised by an FHA-approved appraiser, and the property has to meet minimum standards. All necessary home repairs must be made prior to closing, or the funds will be held in escrow until the repairs are made.

Federal Housing Administration Loan Limits

FHA loans do have limits based on the region. In general, the maximum loan HUD will give out is capped at 115% of the median home price for the county. HUD appraisers will determine the values of homes in that area before giving out the loan.

Federal Housing Administration (FHA) Loan Relief

1. For those who do get an FHA loan, some borrowers may also be eligible for loan relief if they have experienced financial hardship, such as increased living expenses or job loss.

Advantages and Disadvantages of FHA Loans

1. For certain borrowers who cannot get a conventional loan, an FHA loan is an alternative.

2. FHA loans usually do not require high credit scores or low debt-to-income ratio

3. The loan is also federally backed, meaning it is easier to obtain from lenders

Negatives of FHA loans

1. The downside is that these loans come with higher interest rates, and you must purchase PMI

2. Plus, the FHA loan is only for the purchase of a first home and not for a second home or investment property

3. The borrower must purchase private mortgage insurance

4. Finally, not all properties may qualify for an FHA loan

5. The upfront fee for the FHA loan is 1.75% of the total value of the loan, and the monthly fee is based on the value of the home.

Chapter 7: Dodd-Frank Act

The Dodd-Frank Wall Street Reform and Consumer Protection Act legislation was passed by <u>Congress in 2010</u> in response to the financial industry's behavior that led to the housing crisis of 2007–2008. It sought to make the US financial system safer for consumers and taxpayers.

The law, named after its sponsors, Sen. Christopher J. Dodd and Rep. Barney Frank, contains numerous provisions that <u>ensure safe lending practices.</u> Before 2007, the lax regulations in the lending industry led to the housing sector bubble that eventually burst and set off a global crisis. Many financial institutions require government bailout money.

The Dodd-Frank Act was enacted to ensure that no financial crisis event would occur again in the housing market.

Components of the Dodd-Frank Act

1. Financial stability. Under the Dodd-Frank Act, the financial stability of all major lenders would be monitored by the Orderly Liquidation Authority and the Financial

Stability Oversight Council. The law also provides for restructuring or liquidation via the orderly liquidation fund. Further, the council has the legal authority to break up large banks that pose a system risk. Finally, it also forces banks to boost their reserve requirements.

2. The Consumer Financial Protection Bureau (CFPB), established under the Dodd-Frank Act, was tasked with the job of preventing predatory mortgage lending and assisting consumers in understanding the fundamentals of a mortgage before signing on for a loan. More importantly, the <u>CFPM prohibits mortgage brokers from earning high commissions on closing loans</u> with high fees or high-interest rates. In addition, it also requires that mortgage originators not steer potential home buyers to lenders that offer high-interest rates. The CFPM also monitors several other types of consumer lending practices, including debit and credit cards, and addresses consumer complaints. It requires that lenders fully disclose information to consumers in easy-to-read terminology.

3. The <u>Volcker rule</u> limits how financial institutions invest, not participate in proprietary trading and not speculate on trading. Further, banks are not permitted to be involved with private equity firms or hedge firms that are traditionally considered to be high-risk.

4. The Act also has a provision for overseeing features like <u>credit default swaps</u> that were partly also responsible for playing a role in the 2007-2008 financial upheaval.

5. The Dodd-Frank Act also led to the creation of the <u>SEC Office of Credit Rating</u> because, in the past, credit rating agencies were accused of providing false and misleading ratings. The Office of Credit Rating is responsible for ensuring that credit companies/agencies offer reliable, accurate, and meaningful credit ratings of the municipalities, commercial businesses, and other establishments that it assesses.

6. The Dodd-Frank Act also expanded and strengthened the <u>Whistleblower program.</u> Specifically, the Act made it mandatory that whistleblowers can receive anywhere from <u>10 to 30 percent of the proceeds</u> from litigation settlements. Plus, the Act extended the

statute of limitations for whistleblowers to make a claim from 90 to 180 days after a violation is observed.

During the Trump Presidency in 2018, significant features of the Dodd-Frank Act were rolled back to prevent stifling of the financial industry; the Dodd-Frank Act was <u>then replaced by the Economic Growth, Regulatory Relief, and Consumer Protection Act.</u>

Criticism of the Dodd-Frank Act

The biggest criticism of the Dodd-Frank act was that it was <u>harming the competitiveness</u> of US forms compared to their foreign counterparts. The reason was that American firms faced many regulatory compliance requirements, which placed an undue burden on the banks and lenders.

The Key Aim of the Dodd-Frank Act

The key reason for the introduction of the Dodd-Frank act was to reduce the extreme risk in the financial industry. The goal was to protect consumers from outrageous practices such as predatory lending.

The Dodd-Frank is much diluted today chiefly due to the passage of the Economic Growth, Regulatory Relief, and Consumer Protection Act of 2018.

The one downside of the Dodd-Frank Act is that it limited the competitiveness of US firms against their foreign counterparts. The critic felt that too much regulatory compliance placed an undue burden on the financial industry.

The Final Point

The Dodd-Frank Act of 2010 was enacted as an answer to the major financial crisis of 2007–2008, which resulted in massive government bailouts of hundreds of financial lenders and banks under the <u>Troubled Asset Relief Program (TARP).</u>

The Dodd-Frank Act led to numerous reforms in the entire financial sector with the goal of preventing a repeat of the 2007–2008 crisis and the need for additional bailouts by the government. The Act also improved protection for consumers when dealing with lenders and banks, but it also led to decreased growth of the financial sector.

While the Trump administration did weaken and reverse many of the features of the Dodd-Frank Act, mainly those that protected consumers, President Biden again made some additional changes to protect consumers from predatory lenders and abusive practices in the financial industry.

Chapter 8: SAFE Act

The Secure and Fair Enforcement for Mortgage Licensing Act ("SAFE Act") was the government's response to the mortgage crisis of 2008. The Act was created to <u>establish minimum standards for the regulation and licensing of mortgage loan originators</u>. The key aim was to boost consumer protection and decrease fraud in the lending industry.

The Act passed in July 2008 but since then has been overseen by the Consumer Financial Protection Bureau (CFPB), the agency also enforces the Act.

The SAFE Act Features

Without exception, each and every residential mortgage loan originator must be registered, licensed, and covered under a mortgage surety bond. In addition, all mortgage loan originators must also:

• Pass the written exam

• Take continuing education courses

- Complete pre-licensure education courses

- Submit a credit report during the licensure

- Undergo a criminal background check using fingerprints when applying for licensure

The mortgage or loan companies must have some type of financial responsibility built into their state licensing system that meets the minimum standards and national definition that include the following:

- Criminal history and background checks

- Pre-licensure education

- Pre-licensure training

- Continuing education

The Goal of The SAFE Act

The SAFE Mortgage Licensing Act was created to <u>enhance consumer protection and reduce fraud.</u>

The SAFE Act establishes minimum standards for licensing and registration of mortgage loan originators, the American Association of Residential Mortgage Regulators (AARMR), and the Conference of State Bank Supervisors (CSBS).

The objectives of the SAFE Act include the following:

1. Collecting and enhancing the flow of information to and from regulators

2. Enhance customer protection

3. Providing more accountability and monitoring of MLOs

4. Supporting anti-fraud measures

5. Providing consumers with easily accessible information regarding the employment history and enforcement actions against MLOs at no charge

---

Effects of the SAFE Act

1. Most of the changes due to the SAFE ACT relate to <u>specific bond requirements.</u>

2. One change was the addition <u>of tiered bonding requirements</u>. This requirement states that as mortgage companies grow and create a larger volume of loans, the amount of surety bonds also needs to increase.

The SAFE Mortgage Licensing Act also led to the <u>creation of the NMLS (Nationwide Mortgage Licensing System).</u> NMLS consolidates mortgage licensing information in one location and has become a repository for all nationwide licensing in the mortgage industry.

Chapter 9: Consumer Financial Protection Bureau (CFPB)

1. The CFPB is an agency that helps <u>prevent deceptive, unfair, and abusive practices</u> by lenders. For those breaking the law, CFPB usually takes legal action.

2. To ensure fair practice, CFPB regularly empowers and advises Americans on how to watch out for fraud in the lending industry and make sound financial decisions.

3. The <u>CFPB was created during the great recession of 2007-2008</u>, and this was followed by the enactment of the Dodd-Frank Wall Street Reform and Consumer Protection Act in July 2010.

The CFPB is a governmental agency that employs more than 1,500 people in six divisions that include:

- Consumer Education and Engagement

- Enforcement and Fair Lending

- External Affairs

- Legal and Operations.

- Research, Markets, and Regulations

- Supervision

However, the main role of the <u>CFPB is to protect consumers against deceptive, unfair,</u> or abusive practices by lenders. It enforces the law via current consumer financial protection laws.

A brief history of the CFPB

During the great recession in 2007- 2008, it was noted by the government that the financial agencies were not well regulated, nor did the government have strong authority over them, and this was the primary reason for the near economic collapse 16 years ago. Congress then created CFPB to fix those deficiencies.

<u>The CFPB was launched by Senator Elizabeth Warren, and AG Richard Cordray</u> who was its first director.

Why the CFPB is important

Data indicate that nearly 20% of Americans have fallen victim to some type of financial scam in recent years. While in many cases, these scams are handled by local law enforcement, it requires a much broader approach to target scammers who work in many states and sometimes are not even in the USA.

Today credit unions and banks are overseen by a number of federal agencies, including the NCUA, FDIC, and the federal reserve. The CFPB also keeps an eye on credit unions and banks but also covers many other financial products, including monitoring of companies that fall outside the scope of regulators.

All payday loans, credit cards, mortgages, loans, and other financial services offer opportunities for unfair practice and fraud. The 2007-2008 financial crisis is a classic example of massive fraud against Americans, and most got away for free.

Hence besides the CFPB, there are other financial regulators like the Securities and Exchange Commission, which focuses on the stock market and securities, and the Federal Trade Commission, that ensure that there are no deceptive, anti-competitive, or unfair business practices.

Submitting a complaint to the CFPB

Consumers who feel that they have been defrauded can file a complaint with CFPB online. The majority of complaints get a timely response.

Chapter 10: Department of Housing and Urban Development (HUD)

HUD, also referred to as the Department of Housing and Urban Development, is a governmental agency created nearly half a century ago when President Lyndon Johnson decided to fight the lack of home ownership and poverty in the US.

The HUD program created several federal agendas to help Americans achieve inclusive and affordable home ownership in urban areas.

The HUD program has seen many changes over the decades and is run by a Secretary appointed by the US President.

Besides making housing affordable, the HUD Secretary also manages several public programs and supervises the Federal Housing Administration with help for the development of local communities and assisting Americans struggling with rent.

Today, the HUD Secretary also supervises and manages the Federal Housing Administration (FHA), which was created by Congress in 1934.

The FHA is most renowned for its mortgage insurance program, which allows potential homeowners to obtain an FHA home loan when they would otherwise not be eligible for the traditional mortgage due to a prior history of foreclosure, low credit score, failure to pay bills, or not having any down payment.

Fair Housing Act

One of the programs that HUD oversees is the Fair Housing Act which was passed in 1968.

The Fair Housing Act oversees the majority of the residential market and also bars discrimination based on skin color, race, religion, national origin, marital status, age, or disability when borrowers apply for mortgages.

Through the FHA, HUD helps home buyers who do not qualify for loans through conventional lenders; the FHA runs a mortgage insurance program that offers those with bad credit and low incomes the ability to qualify for government-secured FHA loans.

What are HUD Homes?

In general, HUD homes are homes that have been foreclosed and first purchased with FHA loans. A residential property will become a HUD home when the homeowner is unable to keep up with the monthly mortgage and defaults on loan, resulting in foreclosure. The FHA then takes over, repays any outstanding loan balance to the bank/lender, and confiscates the property from the homeowner.

To recover the cost, HUD usually sells homes at below-market prices. The key reason for the low prices is to attract many home buyers and sell the home ASAP. While HUD homes are usually appraised to determine their value and priced accordingly, they are sold as is-. which means no improvements or repairs are made prior to them being sold.

HUD Assistance And Home Buyer Programs

To encourage first-time home buyers to purchase HUD property, the agency does offer several types of incentives that include vouchers, grants, and buyer programs for potential home buyers. Some of the incentives that HUD offers include the following:

1. <u>Housing Choice Voucher Program (also referred to as Section 8):</u> This program allows families with low income, seniors, and those with a disability to obtain homeownership by offering them a regular subsidy in terms of a voucher that enables them to make the monthly mortgage premiums. The local public housing officers review the applicants for vouchers; the great thing is that the home does not have to be part of a subsidized housing project.

2. <u>One Dollar Program</u> permits low to moderate-income families to buy HUD homes that have been on the market for more than 180 days. These homes only cost $1.

3. <u>The Good Neighbor Next Door Program</u> was created to assist public servants like law enforcement officers, teachers, firefighters, and emergency medical personnel purchase homes by offering them 50% off the home's purchase price. Many of these homes can be found in revitalization areas.

4. The <u>Non-profit programs</u> permit religious, non-profit charities, and other communities to purchase HUD homes with a 30% discount. Most of these homes have undergone repairs, and some may need more work before they are habitable. The homes are ideal for low-income families and first-time home buyers.

5. The <u>HUD $100 Down Program</u> makes it possible for some people to own a home by just making a downpayment of $100. However, the buyer must have a steady job and show that he or she will be able to make the mortgage payments.

What to expect with a HUD home?

Buying a HUD home comes with its complexities, and the buyer needs to consider the following:

1. Eligibility: Essentially, any home buyer with funds or one who qualifies for a mortgage is eligible to purchase a HUD home. Some real estate investors may also purchase these homes, but HUD homes are usually meant for owner-occupant buyers, meaning that the buyer will reside in the home and make it the primary residence. The other rule is that the buyer should not have bought another HUD home over the past 24 months. Finally, the last criterion for HUD ownership is that the buyer will remain a resident in the newly purchased home for the first twelve months.

2. Location of homes: It is important to know that HUD homes are not listed on the usual MLS or other home listings. These homes are usually listed on HUD's website- hudhomestore.com.

3. HUD homes are also sold at private auctions. However, in order to view and bid on these homes, one needs to hire a HUD-approved real estate agent.

4. Potential buyers are allowed to make bids over a 30-day period. Following this, HUD reviews all the bids and selects the highest offer. If none of these offers are deemed to be high enough, the bidding program is extended and then opened to investors also. Those with the winning bid are contacted by HUD to settle the buying process. Typically buyers are given 30-60 days to close.

HUD Home Financing

Financing a HUD property is not that different from purchasing any other home since buyers have all the financial options available. While buyers are at liberty to buy a HUD home with the traditional loan secured by Freddie Mac or Fannie Mae, there are several other purchasing options. Veterans who qualify with current service members and their spouses can also buy HUD homes with assistance from VA loans, while buyers who have low credit scores, limited downpayment, and have struggled financially may opt for FHA loans.

HUD home buyers may also opt to finance the purchase of foreclosed homes using an FHA 203(k) loan. The 203K loan will provide the borrower with an adequate amount of money to both finance the home purchase as well as make any necessary repairs.

For borrowers, it is important to go through all the available financing options since many of these <u>HUD properties need significant repairs and/or renovation to make them habitable</u>. The home inspection will tell you if the property is worth the price and will provide you with some idea as to how much you will need to spend to get the property in liveable condition.

The Pros of Purchasing a HUD Home

1. Affordable due to low price: Since some HUD homes may have been foreclosed, the agency wants a quick sale to recoup the administrative and financial costs. Hence, HUD homes that are foreclosed tend to be relatively cheap and way below the market value for comparable homes.

2. Prefer homeowners to investors: The HUD program is designed primarily for owners who prefer to make the property the primary residence. The potential homebuyer is offered a 30-day window period during which he or she can make a bid on the property for sale at the auction. <u>Investors are rarely given priority over these homes.</u>

3. Assistance with Closing costs: Because many HUD home buyers are low-income, HUD does provide assistance with closing costs. <u>HUD offers up to 5% of the home price to pay for administrative and other closing costs.</u>

4. Low down payment: One of the best features of HUD homes is that buyers only require a <u>low down payment</u>. In some cases, the HUD $100 down program may also help

buyers with down payment issues.

The Cons of Purchasing a HUD Home

1. Need to a HUD-approved agent: For home buyers who wish to see and make a bid on HUD homes, they will need to consult and engage with a real estate agent who is registered with HUD

2. Home is sold "as is": The one major downside to HUD homes is that the agency never negotiates. The As-Is homes are sold exactly in the condition shown. For some novice buyers, this may not prove to be a wise move as the home may prove to be unliveable.

3. Residency requirements: All HUD home buyers need to reside in the home for at least the first twelve months. In addition, the buyer is not allowed to buy another HUD property for at least 24 months after the first purchase.

What exactly is a HUD Home?

A HUD home is a property that has been purchased with an FHA-insured mortgage; the previous homeowner most likely failed to repay the mortgage and foreclosed on the home.

These properties are put for sale at an auction where homebuyers can make a bid as long as they intend to make it their primary residence. The homes are usually sold for less than the market value.

Qualifications for a HUD Home

Any individual who can obtain financing for a HUD home is eligible to bid on the property. HUD gives preference to owners who will make the home their primary residence; Investors are almost not given any priority. Assistance from a HUD-registered real estate agent is needed to make a bid. The property usually remains on the auction list for 30 days.

HUD Homes: The Final Point

For Americans who have priced out of the real estate market or that the property market is very competitive, a HUD home may be an option to consider. However, since these properties are foreclosed and sold as is, the buyer needs to do a lot of leg work so that he or she does not purchase a lemon. Once in a while, a HUD home may be of value, but more often than not, they do need extensive repairs and renovation.

Chapter 11: What Is the Fair Housing Act?

The Fair Housing Act was created in 1968 to prevent discrimination in the sale, purchase, financing, or renting of property- public or private based on skin color, race, nationality, sex, or religion. The Fair Housing Act is also known as Title VIII of the Civil Rights Act of 1968.

Over the past 50 years, the statute has been modified and also added family status and disability. While state laws do vary on these protections, they may expand on them but do not have the legal authority to reduce the protections.

The Fair Housing Act is legally enforced at the federal level by the Dept of Housing and Urban Development.

Understanding the Fair Housing Act

The HUD website provides additional information for consumers as to what constitutes discrimination under the law and how the individual should proceed if he or she feels they have been discriminated against.

If discrimination is suspected, the Dept of Justice may file a lawsuit against the landlord or owner of the building, lender, bank, etc. In general, one has to show that there is a pattern of discriminatory practice in order to win the lawsuit.

In some cases, the DOJ will institute criminal charges if a threat of force is used to discriminate.

The victims can file discrimination complaints with CFPB or HUD or file a lawsuit in federal court. In all cases, when a complaint is filed, HUD will investigate and try to resolve it through conciliation.

The person filing a discrimination complaint may elect to file in a federal or state court. If a federal court is selected, the individual is represented by DOJ lawyers. If the case is won, one can receive both punitive and compensatory damages.

Or if the individual seeks an administrative hearing, the representation is by HUD lawyers. This is a faster method compared to the federal trial, but the awards are only limited to compensatory damages. Those who have the money can even hire private real estate attorneys for representation.

Suspecting Discrimination

In general, proving discrimination in housing can be difficult, according to civil rights and housing attorneys. Evidence has to be presented in written text, and hence the borrower needs to get hold of the documents that the lender has- which is not always easy. However, borrowers who feel strongly that they have been discriminated against should contact an attorney or consult with the local fair housing center for guidance.

Chapter 12: The Real Estate Settlement Procedures Act (RESPA)

1. The Real Estate Settlement Procedures Act (RESPA) was passed by the U.S. Congress in <u>1975</u> to provide sellers and homebuyers with complete settlement cost disclosures.

2. RESPA was also enacted to <u>eliminate fraudulent and deceptive practices</u> in the real estate settlement process, restrict the use of an unlimited number of escrow accounts and prohibit kickbacks.

3. RESPA is a federal statute now <u>regulated by the Consumer Financial Protection Bureau (CFPB).</u>

4. RESPA applies to most financial transactions, refinances, purchase loans, home equity lines of credit, and property improvement loans

5. The Act <u>bars lenders from asking for large escrow accounts</u> and limits sellers from mandating title insurance companies.

6. <u>Victims have up to 12 months to file a lawsuit</u> to enforce violations when improper behavior has occurred.

7. The plaintiff has up to 36 months to file a lawsuit against their loan service provider.

8. Initially, the enforcement was by HUD, but after 2011, the legal duties were assumed by CFPB because of the Consumer Protection Act and Dodd-Frank Wall Street Act.

9. The eventual goal of RESPA is to educate consumers regarding the costs of settlement, referral fees, and getting rid of kickback practices.

RESPA Requirements

1. Requires all mortgage brokers, lenders, and servicers of loans to fully disclose to the borrower all information about the loans for a home

2. The disclosure should include relevant consumer protection laws, settlement services, and all other financial information connected to the cost of the real estate settlement process.

3. Any business relationships between other parties and closing service providers connected to the settlement process must be disclosed to the borrower.

RESPA <u>does permit an exception</u> where agents and brokers can exchange reasonable fees in return for services or goods provided by other settlement service providers as long as these transactions are legally compliant and follow regulatory guidelines.

RESPA <u>does not bar joint marketing</u> between a lender and a real estate broker as long as the advertising costs paid by each party are related to the value of service of goods that might be received in return. However, transactions where one party earns more than a prorated of the advertising costs, are banned. In addition, sponsoring events where one party advertises its services is also prohibited.

Lenders are not permitted to force borrowers to use a specific affiliate settlement service provider unless the borrower is provided with financial incentives like a discounted rate.

Types of Real Estate Loans Exempt From RESPA Requirements

RESPA covers all loans backed by the government given out for the purchase of residential properties designed for one to four families. This includes purchase loans, refinances, and reverse mortgages.

The loan can even be used to improve or purchase a rental property of one to four residential units.

RESPA does not apply to loans for commerce, business, agricultural properties, investments

If a loan is obtained to purchase vacant land, but none of the loan proceeds are used to contract a covered residential structure, the loan is exempt from RESPA oversight.

Certain Loan Assumptions

When a Loan is assumed, the bank or lender has no authority to approve future individuals for the assumption; otherwise, the loan is not covered by RESPA. Except for the VA loan, most residential loans are not assumable.

Construction-Only Loans

In most cases. RESPA does not cover construction loans

Are Reverse Mortgages Covered by RESPA?

Reverse mortgages, like the primary mortgage, are covered by RESPA. At the time of the application, the lender has an obligation to disclose specific details about the mortgage, the total cost of the loan, and any relationships with service providers.

All disclosures for the most common type of reverse mortgage (HECM) have to be done with the <u>HUD-1 Settlement Statement</u>, which is a slightly different disclosure form compared to the traditional mortgage.

Chapter 13: The Equal Credit Opportunity Act

The Equal Credit Opportunity Act (ECOA) is a federal civil rights law enacted in 1974 that forbids lenders, including financial institutions, to <u>discriminate against loan borrowers</u> for any personal reason other than their ability to repay.

More specifically, ECOA protects all borrowers of loans from discrimination based on race, religion, national origin, color, age, sexual discrimination, marital status, religion, eligibility for public assistance, or exercising any rights under the Consumer Credit Protection Act.

The Dept of Justice can file lawsuits under ECOA if there is evidence of a pattern of discrimination involving any type of home mortgage loan.

The ECOA is supported by several federal agencies to help enforce the law, chiefly by the Consumer Financial Protection Bureau (CFPB)

ECOA prohibits discrimination against all types of credit transactions and applies to any lender, including small loan and finance companies, banks, credit unions, credit card companies, and retail stores.

ECOA covers many types of credits, including:

• Credit cards

• Personal loans

• Small business loans

• Student loans

• Car loans

• Loan modifications

And ECOA does not only apply to consumer loans but to corporations, small businesses, trusts, and partnerships.

Special Considerations

Lenders often ask for personal facts from borrowers who apply for credit. While obtaining many of these personal facts is prohibited by ECOA, answering them is optional, and the lender cannot use them to make a decision on a loan.

ECOA also allows each spouse in a marriage to have their own credit history. But if the borrower has a joint account, the credit report will show both names. This means that a spouse's financial behavior can negatively or positively impact the borrower's credit score.

What Happens if You are Turned Down for a Loan?

1. If the borrower has been denied a loan or line of credit, the lender may reveal to you in

the <u>Adverse Action Notice</u> the exact reason why the application was rejected.

2. Consumers have the legal right to ask the reason for a loan denial <u>within 60 days</u> of receiving the rejection notification from the creditor.

3. Even though ECOA prohibits lenders from making decisions on some loans, sometimes the lender may ask the borrower to disclose if he or she is relying on child support or alimony income to obtain credit. However, the borrower cannot be denied a loan simply because they are divorced.

Your ECOA Rights

When consumers apply for a line of credit or loan, they are given the following rights:

1. When borrowers apply for credit, only relevant financial factors like credit score, credit history, and income are taken into account.

2. All borrowers are entitled to have credit in their birth name, first name, spouse's last name, or a combination of two last names.

3. Even if you change your marital status or name, you can keep the account unless you are unable to pay

4. <u>The creditor must inform you within 30 days whether your application was approved or not.</u>

5. If the borrower's application is rejected, the lender has to provide a specific reason within 60 days.

What Lenders Cannot Do?

1. Cannot impose different conditions or a term like higher interest rates based on your personal features

2. Cannot bar you from loans just because you receive reliable public assistance

3. When you apply for an unsecured loan, the lender is not supposed to ask you about your marital status or ask if you are divorced or a widower.

Detecting the Signs of Credit Discrimination

Credit discrimination is not always easy to detect, and thus, consumers need to watch out for these ECOA violations:

• You are promised the loan on the phone, but when you arrive in person, things change

• The lender discourages you from applying for any type of loan

• The lender may make negative remarks about national origin, marital status, gender, etc

• Even though you meet all the criteria, you are refused the loan

• Even though you qualify for a low-interest loan, you are offered a loan with very high-interest rates

• You are denied a loan without a reasonable explanation

• The lender aggressively pushes you into signing for a loan that just does not seem right

What to Do if You Suspect Discrimination

For consumers who feel they have been discriminated against, there are some things they can do:

• First, contact the lender to complain. Sometimes this may persuade the lender to relook at your application for a loan.

• Check with your state's Attorney General's office to see if the creditor has violated any state equal credit opportunity laws.

• If any violations are suspected, they should be reported to the appropriate government agency. If the borrower has been denied credit for no valid reason, then the creditor will also be required to provide a statement to the particular government agency.

• Most borrowers initiate the process by submitting a complaint to the Consumer Financial Protection Bureau. Once the complaint is received, the CFPB tries to determine if there is a pattern of discrimination by the lender, the number of people who have been affected, and what other fair lending laws have been violated.

• The victim does have the option to sue the lender in a federal district court. If the lender is found to be guilty of discrimination or in violation of other laws, the victim may be eligible for both actual and punitive damages.

Who Supports the Equal Credit Opportunity Act (ECOA)?

To ensure compliance with the law, the Consumer Financial Protection Board writes the rules to implement ECOA. In addition, other federal agencies also share the job of ensuring compliance, including the following:

• Federal Deposit Insurance Corporation (FDIC)

• Federal Reserve Board (FRB)

• National Credit Union Administration (NCUA)

• Office of the Comptroller of the Currency (OCC)

Penalty for Violating the Equal Credit Opportunity Act (ECOA)

Creditors and lenders who violate ECOA can potentially face class action lawsuits from the Dept of Justice. If found guilty, the creditor or lender will face punitive damages and any costs that have been incurred by the borrower.

Does ECOA Apply to All Lenders?

The Equal Credit Opportunity Act applies to all lenders and banks. Financial institutions, including private lenders, who have the job of giving out mortgages do not have the legal right to discriminate against applicants based on personal features. In addition, lenders and other related workers should not discourage or deter consumers from seeking or applying for a loan from elsewhere.

Chapter 14: Additional Important Laws

The Gramm-Leach-Bliley Act

1. The Gramm-Leach-Bliley Act (GLBA) of 1999 was a bi-partisan regulation that became active under President Bill Clinton and was passed by Congress on November 12, 1999.

2. The key goal of GLBA was to modernize and update the financial industry. The GLBA is most well known for its repeal of the Glass Steagall Act of 1933. The latter law did not permit commercial banks to offer a range of financial services like insurance and other investments as part of normal operations. In simple terms, banks were not legally allowed to function as brokers.

3. Under the GLBA, each service person or manager was only permitted to manage or sell only one type of financial instrument or product.

4. Finally, all lenders/banks must reveal to the customer their information-sharing practices. The goal was to permit customers the option of canceling or opting out if they did not want any of their personal information shared

In summary, the Gramm Leach Bliley Act ensured limited privacy protection for customers by preventing the sharing of personal data among banks.

National Housing Act of 1934

1. As part of President Roosevelt's New Deal, the National Housing Act (NHA) was passed in 1934 to support the construction of homes and improve the residential housing market.

2. The nation was in despair during the great depression, and it was hoped that this Act would boost the recovery efforts.

3. The National Housing Act led to the creation of the Federal Housing Administration, which instituted a mortgage insurance program backed by the federal government. The FHA-backed insurance would lower the risk for banks and lenders, who could then make mortgages available to Americans who otherwise would not qualify for homeownership. The FHA program proved to be robust and still exists today, providing affordable mortgage options to buyers of single and multi-family homes.

American Recovery and Reinvestment Act of 2009

Following the 2008 Financial crisis and subprime mortgage meltdown, the US government tried to kickstart the economy with the passage of the American Recovery and Reinvestment Act in 2009. The government-funded an $800 billion stimulus package, of which nearly $14 billion was devoted to the housing market. Of that, $4 billion was awarded to HUD for modernizing and repairing public homes, $2 billion went towards section 8 housing rental assistance, and another $1.5 billion was set aside for rental assistance in an effort to counter homelessness.

Chapter 15: The 1003 Mortgage Application Form

1. Anyone who applies for a mortgage today will be expected to complete the 1003 <u>Mortgage application form</u>.

2. The 1003 mortgage application, also referred to as the Uniform Residential Loan Application, is currently the standard document that has to be completed when applying for a loan in the US.

3. The borrower will complete this particular form or its equivalent, known as Form 65, when applying for a mortgage.

4. Some lenders continue to use alternative mortgage application forms or accept the basic form from the borrower to understand their finances, the value of the property, and the type of property. However, for the most part, the 1003 form has now become the standard in the lending industry.

5. <u>Form 1003 is mandatory</u> when one applies for a mortgage from the Federal National Mortgage Association (Fannie Mae) and the Federal Home Loan Mortgage Corporation

(Freddie Mac)

Form 1003 asks the usual questions about the borrower, including:

- Employment history

- Income

- Assets

- Debts

- Type of property

- Value of the property

Form 1003 is usually completed twice during the mortgage application; the first time is during the initial application and again when closing.

The 1003 Loan Application Form was developed by the Federal National Mortgage Association, or Fannie Mae, as a standardized form for the industry. Because mortgages need to be well documented, this is where form 1003 is helpful; it is easy to complete and understand for both the borrower and lender and helps simplify the process of mortgage processing.

In March 2021, form 1003 was redesigned, and all new applications must use this updated form.

Form 1003 collects all the relevant information from the borrower to deem whether he or she is a risk for a loan. Here is a list of things that are needed on the form:

- Employment history- at least two years and monthly income

- Any other household income

• Itemized list of liabilities (current mortgage, rent, car loans, student loans, credit card debt

• Itemized list of assets (life insurance policy, saving and checking accounts, stocks, bonds, IRA or similar accounts, pension, child support, alimony

• Does the borrower own any other property or a second home?

• What is the value and type of property the borrower wishes to buy now? Is it a rental property, and how much rent will be earned every month?

Once the form is completed, the borrower has to sign it and give permission to the lender to perform a credit check.

In summary, form 1003 has nine sections that need to be completed.

Completing form 1003 does require a little time, but it is now required when applying for a mortgage in the US. Because of its universality, form 1003 has made it easier for lenders to evaluate the creditworthiness of borrowers. For those who are considering a mortgage, take some time out and check your credit rating to see if you will qualify got a loan- it will save you a lot of hassles.

Chapter 16: Seller Financing

Sometimes during the home purchase, the seller may agree to do the financing instead of a bank or a private lender. Also known as owner financing, the buyer signs a mortgage with the seller. In most cases, <u>seller financing will include a balloon payment 2- 5 years</u> after the property sale.

How does Seller Financing Work?

Some buyers may have great difficulty obtaining a conventional loan either due to poor credit or job instability. And for these individuals, seller financing may be an option. <u>Unlike the traditional lender or bank, seller financing usually is less bureaucratic and involves no or very few costs</u>. Sometimes there may not even be an appraisal fee. Plus, unlike lenders, sellers are more flexible when it comes to the amount of downpayment. Most importantly, seller financing is a much faster process, and the entire process can be completed within 5-7 days.

<u>One of the major downsides of seller financing is that if the buyer suddenly stops the</u> <u>payment, the seller may incur a heavy loss as well as exorbitant legal fees.</u>

For sellers, sometimes financing the buyer's mortgage can make the process of home sale faster and easier. This is especially true when there is a down in the real estate market, and then obtaining credit is difficult. For the seller, the advantage is that they can get a premium for offering to finance and are more likely to get the asking price for the home in a buyer's market.

Seller financing fluctuates in popularity depending on the overall difficulty of getting a mortgage. During times when lenders are leery of giving out loans and will only lend money to the most creditworthy borrowers, seller financing can make it possible for some people to buy homes.

Seller financing also makes it easier to sell a property. <u>On the other hand, when the credit market is loose, and the banks are readily lending money even to people with low credit scores, seller financing usually has low appeal to home buyers.</u>

But like a bank or lender, sellers also face similar risks of borrower default, and they must be fully aware of it.

Negatives of Seller Financing

The one major negative for <u>buyers is that they will most likely have to pay higher interest rates</u> than if they elected to obtain a mortgage from a bank.

Lenders and banks tend to have more flexibility in offering interest rates to credit-worthy customers. If you elect to go with seller financing, in the long term, the high-interest rates will use up all the savings that you earned from avoiding the closing costs. On top of that, the onus is on the buyer to prove he or she has the ability to repay the loan.

Plus, the buyer will need to fork out more money to perform a title search and ensure that it is free from encumbrances. Other charges may include document stamps, survey fees, and taxes.

For the seller, if the buyer does not pay the loan, the only remedy is to go to court, but that will not matter if the buyer has foreclosed. In most cases, the seller will have a clause in the mortgage that has a due on sale or an alienation clause. These clauses require full repayment of the current mortgage when the property sells. What this means is that both the buyer and seller need to work with an experienced real estate attorney to draft the paperwork, cover up all the negative possibilities and close the deal, but remember, these lawyers do not come cheap.

Chapter 17: Real Estate Closing

The final step when purchasing a home is closing. This is a necessary step that ensures that the property now belongs to the borrower. However, before closing can occur, the borrower needs to take care of a few things.

1. Consult with a real estate lawyer: for most people, a home purchase is the single largest item they will ever buy, and in order to preserve the asset, it is important to work with a lawyer who can help with the paperwork and guide you through the process. In general, an <u>experienced real estate lawyer will cost anywhere from $800-$1,500.</u> In most states, there is a mandatory requirement to hire a lawyer during the closing.

2. Open an Escrow Account for safety. In general, an escrow account is overseen by a third party on behalf of the seller and buyer. The escrow account reduces the risk of fraud since all the money is held by a neutral third party. The money is only released to the seller when everything is settled.

3. Title and insurance: to safeguard your investment, your lawyer must conduct a search for the home's title and insurance. This is to ensure that no one else can later claim the property. The title search will examine public records to confirm the legal ownership of the property. It will also reveal any claims that exist against the property. If there are, they need to be resolved before signing the contract.

4. Title insurance helps protect the buyer from any financial loss in cases there is a defect in the property title. It also protects lenders and real estate owners against losses that may occur as a result of encumbrances, liens, or title defects.

5. Learn to negotiate. Buying a home is not a cheap undertaking, and there are many fees involved that can quickly snowball. From home and pest inspection to the hiring of a lawyer, you have to pay the fees. Sometimes the lender may impose junk fees at the time of closing, which includes administrative fees, photocopying fees, application eve fees, processing fees, and so on. So get to know the average cost of the fees so that you don't get ripped off. In real estate, prices tend to get inflated, and deception is rampant. Often if you speak up, you may be able to get the junk fees removed.

6. Don't forget the home inspection: Before the contract signing, the onus is on the buyer to ensure that the home has been inspected for any potential problems. If any issues are found, the buyer must tell the seller to fix them or offer a discount on the home price.

7. Pest inspection, like the home inspection, is necessary to ensure that there are no wood-destroying insects in the home. Pest can quickly damage the home structure, making it inhabitable. Today, many lenders mandate that all minor pest issues be fixed before closing. In some states, pest inspections are mandatory.

8. Repairs: If the home is in need of repair, perhaps you may want to renegotiate the price of the home. If the seller is eager to get rid of the home, he or she may agree to a lower price.

9. Fixed interest rate: If you are buying a home at a time when the interest rates are low, lock in your interest rate. However, other factors that will determine low-interest

rates include your credit score, the location of the home, the type of loan, and the property type. Locking in low-interest rates can be extremely beneficial when making monthly premium mortgage payments.

10. Earnest money: In most cases, when a home buyer likes a property, he or she will put down a deposit or otherwise known as earnest money. To the seller, this indicates seriousness, good faith, and genuine interest in the real estate deal. If the buyer rescinds the offer, the seller gets to keep the earnest money; if the seller backs out, the money is returned to the buyer.

11. To complete the home purchase, the borrower will have to place additional funds into the escrow, which will go toward the down payment.

12. Add contingencies to the contract: Your real estate offer should be contingent on the following features:

• That the borrower can obtain financing at an interest rate that is affordable

• The home inspection has not revealed any major deficits

• The seller has been transparent and fully disclosed known issues with the property

• The pest inspection does not show any damage or major infestation

• The seller agrees to complete all agreed-upon repairs before closing

In some cases, specific dates are added to the contingencies. These contingencies must

be provided to the seller and lender before closing.

13. Walk-through: Before signing the contract, the buyer should perform a final walk-through

of the property to make sure that there is no damage since the last home inspection. At this point, the buyer must verify or check if the requested home repairs have been completed. Finally, check to ensure that nothing included in the contract has been removed, like the air conditioning, HVAC system, etc.

The Actual Closing and Paperwork

All buyers need to know the paperwork they will be signing during closing. This is usually done in the presence of a lawyer and if there are any legal terms you don't understand, ask the lawyer before you sign. Things that you should pay attention to include the agreed-upon interest rate, the amount of the loan, the duration of the loan, etc. Finally, compare the closing costs to the good faith estimate that was given to the borrower at the start of the process; this is the time to despite any fees that you think are deceptive.

Time to Close

Usually, it takes anywhere from 4-6 weeks to close on a home. However, this also depends on the home's location and how fast you can get it inspected and obtain a loan.

The Closing Costs

There are many fees associated with closing besides the lawyer fees. These costs vary from 2-6% of the home's purchase price and are due at closing.

It may seem like closing is a major headache, but it is part of the deal if you want to legitimately own a home. Borrowers showed never signing a deal under pressure and not being pressured into signing anything.

Chapter 18: Home Appraisal

One key component of real estate buying or selling is an appraisal of the property. It is important for both the buyer and seller to understand how appraisal works and how the home value is determined.

The cost of a home appraisal for an average home in the US varies from $250 to $500. The buyer usually pays the appraisal fee.

The important thing about an appraisal is that it must be an unbiased professional opinion of the value of the home.

An appraisal is usually required whenever there is a loan involved in the refinancing, buying, or selling of property.

The appraisal usually requires an in-person inspection that will also include recent sales of similar properties in the area, current market trends, and details of the home that includes its condition, size, amenities, floor plan, and neighborhood.

In the event that the appraisal value of the property is much lower than expected, the buyer may cancel or delay the transaction.

In most cases, the appraisal is used to determine if the home's current price is appropriate given the condition of the home's ocean, condition, and features.

Lenders usually would like to know that the potential homebuyer is not overborrowing since the home serves as collateral for the mortgage. If the borrower defaults on the mortgage and forecloses, the lender will sell the home to recoup the money it loaned. The appraisal helps the lender protect itself against lending more than the actual home's worth.

The appraiser should be certified or licensed and have familiarity with the local community. The appraiser should be free of bias and have no indirect or direct interest in the real estate transaction.

What the Appraiser Looks For

1. It is important to know that the home's appraisal value is greatly influenced by recent transactions involving similar properties and current trends.

2. The appraiser must find out about recent home sales and their price.

3. The appraiser will evaluate the home's amenities and size, including the number of bedrooms and bathrooms and the floor plan's functionality.

4. The appraiser will usually conduct a thorough visual exam of the exterior and interior and look for any features that can adversely affect the property value and/or may need repairs.

5. Once the appraisal is completed, the report is documented using the Uniform Residential Appraisal Report from Fannie Mae for single-family homes.

What the appraisal report should include:

• Location of the appraised property, preferably showing it on a street map

• Sketch of the exterior building

• The square footage and how it was calculated

• Photos of the home's front, rear, and street

• Sales of comparable properties in the area, market sales tax, public tax records, etc

When the borrower is trying to finance a mortgage, if the home equity value by the appraiser is less than 20%, the borrower will be required to purchase PMI.

Appraisals Facts

1. If the appraisal value is around the contract price, the transaction proceeds as planned.

2. If the appraisal is stated to be below the contract price, the transaction may be delayed or canceled.

3. A lender will usually not give out more money if the appraiser values the home to be far above the contract price.

4. Appraisals tend to favor buyers as they help overpay for the home

5. Sellers may not agree with a low appraisal and may refuse to lower the price of the home.

6. Sometimes, a second opinion is needed when the first appraisal is not realistic, or sales of nearby foreclosures and short sales have dragged the home price down.

Practice Test 1

1. What is false about an adjustable rate mortgage?

a. Is a good long-term loan

b. Has interest rates that change

c. Initial monthly payments are low

d. It is considered to be a high-risk loan

Answer A

An adjustable-rate mortgage (ARM) is a loan with changing interest rates. ARMs usually start with low monthly premiums compared to fixed-rate mortgages, but in almost all cases, this changes with time. And as the interest rates change, so does the monthly premium. ARM loans are best for an individual who only wants to finance for a few years and then apply for other means of financing where the interest rates are fixed or predictable.

2. In general, how long do fixed-rate mortgages last?

a. Less than a year

b. Between two to ten years

c. Usually more than 20 years

d. As long as you want

Answer B

Fixed-rate mortgages usually have a duration between one to ten years. If the interest rates are low, most borrowers apply for the longest duration of the loan.

3. What is the most significant advantage of a fixed-rate mortgage?

a. It is a long-term loan

b. Monthly premiums remain the same

c. Interest rates are low

d. It can be canceled anytime without penalty

Answer B

The key advantage of a fixed-rate mortgage is that the monthly mortgage premiums remain the same for the duration of the loan. With a fixed-rate mortgage, the amount one pays towards the mortgage does not change for a specified number of years.

4. In general, the reason why is the loan-to-value ratio of importance?

a. It permits the potential buyer to get a bigger loan

b. It allows the lender to determine the risk of the loan

c. It permits the potential buyer to select his or her lender

d. It allows the lender to determine the size of the down payment

Answer B

The loan-to-value ratio is an essential assessment because it provides the lender with some information about the risk of the loan. If the loan-to-value ratio is high, then this is a red flag for a high-risk loan.

5. What does 70% loan-to-value mean?

a. The buyer will put down a 70% downpayment

b. The buyer will put down at least a 30% deposit

c. The lender will only give a loan of 30%

d. The lender will rescind the offer

Answer B

A 70% loan-to-value mortgage is a loan where the borrower puts down a deposit of at least 30% of the total property value which is being remortgaged or purchased. This means the borrower will need to obtain a mortgage of 70% from the bank or lender.

6. Lenders are usually required to give consumers the Good Faith Estimate documents at what time after closing?

a. Within three days

b. Within the first seven days

c. When the borrower asks for it

d. When the mortgage payments have started

Answer A

By law, the lender must provide the borrower with a good faith estimate document within three days of receiving the loan application. This document will include the total cost of the loan, including title change, taxes, administrative fees, and closing costs.

7. The Good Faith Estimate has been replaced by the?

a. Home loan toolkit

b. Loan estimate

c. Closing settlement document

d. Mortgage loan application document

Answer B

The good faith estimate was once the absolute guide to determine the costs of a loan, but the document has been replaced by the Loan Estimate.

8. During the initial stage of the loan application process, when disclosures have not been made, the lender can only charge the potential borrower with what fee?

a. Home inspection fee

b. Survey fee

c. Credit report fee

d. Consult fee

Answer C

During the initial stage of the loan application, the lender will only charge for the cost of doing a credit check. This may be done several times to ensure that the borrower's financial status has not altered. The cost of a credit check varies from $10 to $100.

9. What is the usual loan origination fee in the USA?

a. 0.5% to 1%

b. 3% to 5%

c. Depends on the property value

d. It depends on the lender

Answer A

An origination fee is usually between 0.5% to 1% of the loan amount. The lender charges this fee for processing the loan application. Sometimes the borrower may be able to negotiate this fee with the lender, but if the fee is waived, the borrower will end up paying high-interest rates over the life of the loan.

10. The loan estimate document will provide the borrower with information on all the below topics except?

a. Closing costs

b. Interest rate

c. Reverse mortgage

d. Costs to buy a home

Answer C

A loan estimate is a three-page document that is given to the borrower by the lender during the process of a loan application. Once the application is submitted, the lender has three days to give the borrower an estimate that details all the costs of purchasing a home, including the interest rates and closing costs. A loan estimate is not given when the borrower applies for a HELOC or a reverse mortgage.

11. In general, mortgage insurance is required when your down payment is?

a. Less than 3%

b. Less than 5%

c. Less than 10%

d. Less than 20%

Answer D

In general, across the country, mortgage loan insurance is required by lenders when the borrower makes a down payment of less than 20% of the home.

12. Regulation B is also known as the:

a. Equal Credit Opportunity Act

b. Truth in lending act

c. Fair housing act

d. Real Estate Settlement Procedures act

Answer A

Regulation B protects consumers and prohibits lenders from discriminating based on age, gender, ethnicity, nationality, or marital status.

13. What is a straw buyer?

a. Someone who only buys small homes

b. Someone who prefers a home that looks like a straw

c. A buyer who purchases property on behalf of someone else

d. A buyer who can only pay cash for the property

Answer C

A straw buyer is an individual who purchases a property in the name of another group, person, or entity which may or may not be part of a fraudulent plan.

14. The SAFE Act primarily refers to mortgage loans for which type of properties?

a. 1-4 non-owner occupied rentals

b. Individual condominiums

c. Motels

d. Schools

Answer B

The SAFE Act usually applies to residential properties and does not apply to real estate investments or commercial buildings.

15. How many hours of continuing education must MLOs complete each year?

a. 8

b.16

c. 20

d. 25

Answer A

All licensed mortgage loan officers are required to take a minimum of eight hours of continuing education every year. In addition, there may also be some specific state requirements to maintain the license.

16. RESPA does not cover which of the following loans?

a. Home equity lines of credit

b. Property improvement loans

c. Seller-financed mortgages

d. Loans on one to four-family residential properties

Answer C

RESPA, in general, applies to all "federally-related" real estate dealings that involve residential properties meant for one to four families. RESPA does not cover all loans, including mortgages for commercial properties, business investments, or agriculture.

17. An affiliate business arrangement is said to exist when a lender owns at least what percentage of a settlement service provider?

a. 1%

b. 5%

c. 25%

d. 50%

Answer A

An Affiliated Business Arrangement is said to exist when the individual in charge of financial services refers the customer to a real estate settlement service in which he or she has a direct financial interest. Even if the individual only has a 1% interest in the settlement business, a referral is not ethical and is considered a violation of RESPA.

18. How do you define appraisal?

a. Refers to the exact cost of a home

b. The cost of building a home

c. The market value of a home

d. Cost of a home following an inspection

Answer C

An appraisal is deemed to be a fair market valuation of an item/property, such as a business, real estate, antique, or collectible. The appraisal is usually done by an authorized professional.

18. After closing, when is the lender supposed to provide the initial escrow statement to the buyer?

a. ASAP

b. Within the first ten days

c. When the borrower asks for it

d. Within 45 days of the closing

Answer D

Once the closing is done, the initial escrow statement is usually given to the borrower at the time of the settlement or within 45 days of closing.

19. The Fair Credit Reporting Act (FRCA) is also known as Regulation?

a. A

b. C

c. Z

d. V

Answer D

Regulation V is a federal Act adopted by the Consumer Financial Protection Bureau. The Regulation ensures that all consumer data reported in a credit report will remain confidential and be protected at all times. The credit report also has to be accurate, as mandated by the Fair Credit Reporting Act.

20. What is true about a balloon mortgage?

a. It amortizes

b. The loan is paid back in a single sum

c. Comes with high-interest rates

d. It is usually a long-term loan

Answer B

A balloon mortgage is a type of property loan where the borrower makes none or very small monthly payments for a short period, usually about five to seven years. A balloon payment mortgage, unlike other mortgages, does not amortize over the duration of the loan. At maturity, the borrower has to repay the balance in one large sum.

21. One of the key reasons why many disclosure laws have been introduced in the lending business is to?

a. Make the consumer well-informed

b. To let the lender know that he or she is being monitored

c. Allow consumers to know the exact costs

d. Allows consumers to choose their service provider

Answer A

Prior to the 2007-2008 housing crisis, the mortgage industry was replete with fraud and deceptive practices. Since the Dodd-Frank Act, many other federal acts have been introduced in the world of loan service providers. The major aim of the disclosure laws is to make sure that the consumer is fully informed about the loan and lender practices.

22. An upfront mortgage insurance premium is often required for which type of loan?

a. USDA

b. VA

c. FHA

d. HUD

Answer C

Unlike many other loans, a residential single-family mortgage from the FHA does require an upfront mortgage insurance premium (MIP). Lenders must see proof of the MIP within ten calendar days of the mortgage closing, or the loan will be canceled.

23. Discrimination by lenders is prohibited by which law?

a. ECOA

b. RESPA

c. FHA

d. Dodd-Frank Act

Answer A

The federal civil rights law or the Equal Credit Opportunity Act (ECOA) is a federal government law that is a federal civil rights law that outlaws banks and private lenders from discriminating against borrowers for any reason other than the ability to repay back the loan. Specifically, the ECOA protects all borrowers from discrimination based on color, race, sex, religion, marital status, age, national origin, or reliance on public assistance.

24. An adverse action notice by the lender has to be submitted within how many days?

a. 7

b. 14

c. 21

d. 30

Answer D

In general, an adverse action notice by the lender must be submitted within 30 days.

25. What does the term 'escalation' mean in relation to a loan?

a. buyer can increase the offer in predetermined amounts whenever someone outbids

b. Buyer can shorten the time for loan closure

c. The seller can ask for rapid payments

d. The lender can perform a background check

Answer A

One of the clauses when making a lease or a real estate offer is the escalation clause. This clause makes it possible for the buyer to increase the offer in predetermined amounts whenever someone outbids the initial buyer. In simple terms, if there is a higher competing offer submitted by someone else, then the original buyer is allowed to increase his or her bid by a certain amount above the offer submitted.

26. What is the defeasance clause in a mortgage?

a. Substitute a collateral loan prepayment plan

b. Another name for fraud in loan servicing

c. Drop in interest rates

d. A home can go to foreclosure if one premium payment is missed

Answer A

Defeasance is a method of lowering the fees necessary when the borrower decides to prepay a fixed-rate commercial real estate loan. The defeasance clause permits the borrower to exchange another cash-flowing asset instead of paying cash to the lender. In simple terms, it is a penalty that involves the substitution of collateral.

27. What does the term escrow mean in real estate?

a. Paying off the mortgage sooner than expected

b. The lender holds the money until the background check is completed

c. It is the same as a security deposit

d. A legal arrangement where a third party holds the money

Answer D

Escrow is a legal maneuver where an independent third-party arrangement will hold property or money for a short term until a specified condition or payment has been fulfilled as per the purchase contract.

28. Once the buyer has paid off the remainder of his mortgage, how many days does the lender have to submit the satisfaction mortgage letter?

a. 10

b. 20

c. 30

d. 60

Answer D

In most states, once the borrower has paid off the mortgage, the lender has 60 days to submit the mortgage satisfaction letter.

29. National flood maps are usually provided by?

a. NASA

b. FDA

c. FEMA

d. Dept of Agriculture

Answer C

For potential home buyers who would like to know if the locality is at risk for flooding, one can obtain flood maps from FEMA. This agency provides flood maps for the entire country.

30. Who usually issues the Certificate of Reasonable value?

a. FHA

b. HUD

c. VA

d. Any lender

Answer C

The Certificate of Reasonable Value is issued by the Veterans Benefits Administration. This certificate is only provided after the home has been inspected by a VA-approved appraiser.

31. The Federal National Mortgage Association is also known as:

a. Freddie Mac

b. Fannie Mae

c. USDA

d. HUD

Both Freddie Mac and Fannie Mae were created by Congress so that they could play a critical role in the nation's financing of homes; Congress hoped that both would bring stability, transparency, and affordability to the mortgage industry. Both Freddie Mac and Fannie Mae do provide funds on reasonable terms to private lenders and banks across the nation. Unfortunately, both agencies functioned poorly, as was evident during the last housing crisis.

32. In general, loans for purchasing property in rural areas are issued by:

a. USDA

b. FDA

c. HUD

d. VA

Answer A

In general, for rural home buyers, USDA loans come with zero-down-payment mortgages. The USDA loans are only for those who are not able to get a traditional mortgage and are not wealthy.

33. What parameter does the income capitalization approach use to determine the market value of the property?

a. Size of the property

b. Location

c. Average offers on the property

d. Income generated

Answer D

The income capitalization approach, also known as the income approach, utilizes the amount of income generated from a property to determine its market value. The income-generated approach is typically utilized for commercial real estate, including apartment buildings, office buildings, and shopping centers.

34. Home Mortgage Disclosure Act is also known as Regulation:

a. C

b. N

c. X

d. Z

Answer A

The Home Mortgage Disclosure Act was enacted in 1975 by Congress. It was then implemented by the Federal Reserve Board and referred to as Regulation C.

35. The USDA loan requires a minimum credit score of?

a. 500

b. 640

c. 700

d. No credit score is required

Answer B

For those applying for a USDA loan, a minimum credit score of 640 is essential. However, the USDA does not only rely on credit scores to approve a loan, and some candidates with lower scores may be eligible for a USDA-backed mortgage.

36. What does the term 'exculpatory' mean in real estate?

a. Clause in the contract where one party limits the other party's liability

b. The borrower has financial liability

c. The lender has financial liability.

d. Both the lender and borrower are deemed financially liable

Answer A

The exculpatory clause in a lease, contract, or loan document is a clause whereby one party limits the other party's liability.

37. How does forbearance apply to your mortgage?

a. Pay the entire mortgage in full ahead of time

b. Intentionally reduce your mortgage payments

c. Put the home in foreclosure and avoid paying the mortgage

d. Ask the lender to pay your mortgage

Answer B

Forbearance is when the lender or mortgage servicer permits the borrower to reduce or pause the payments for a short period of time.

38. What is the minimum credit score required for Fannie Mae?

a. 600

b. 620

c. 650

d. 680

Answer B

To qualify for a loan from Fannie Mae, one has to have a credit score of at least 620. In fact, Fannie Mae prefers to give loans to people with high credit scores

39. What does a loan prospector evaluate?

a. Credit worthiness

b. Criminal history

c. Stable job

d. Experience with a home purchase

Answer A

The role of a Loan Prospector is to assess the credit worthiness of the borrower. After reviewing the borrower's financial and other data, he or she may make a recommendation for an FHA loan eligibility.

40. Which of the following is not true about a loan shark?

a. They are all licensed

b. They charge high-interest rates

c. They sometimes use threats when people do not pay back

d. They usually offer small loans

Answer A

In most cases, loan sharks are unscrupulous and unlicensed money lenders. They usually charge exorbitant interest rates and often use violence and threats to scare people who, unfortunately, are not able to repay the loan.

41. Which of the following is not typical of an amortized loan?

a. Credit card loan

b. Home Mortgage

c. Car loan

d. Student loan

Answer A

The majority of credit card loans are structured as non-amortizing loans. When obtaining a loan with a credit card, instead of paying back the principal on a scheduled payment plan, you only make the monthly minimum payments. Classic examples of amortized loans include car loans, conventional mortgages, and student loans.

42. What is a reverse mortgage?

a. Loan that is obtained without selling the home

b. A loan that is obtained by putting the home in escrow

c. A loan that is obtained by putting the home in foreclosure

d. A loan that comes with no interest

Answer A

A reverse mortgage is a loan that permits the borrower to obtain money from the home equity; there is usually no need to sell the home. But if the money is not repaid, it can quickly lead to repossession by the lender.

43. The Home Mortgage Disclosure Act is also known as Regulation?

a. B

b. C

c. N

d. Z

Answer B

The Home Mortgage Disclosure Act was enacted in 1975 by Congress and later implemented by the Federal Reserve Board is known as Regulation C.

44. If you are going to buy a home with a USDA loan, how much downpayment is necessary?

a. None

b. 3%

c. 10%

d. Minimum of 20%

Answer A

Unlike most other loans, a USDA loan does not require any down payment. However, you still need a minimum credit score of 580 to be eligible for the loan. The USDA loan is for the purchase of property in rural areas.

45. If you are late with your monthly premium on a HUD loan, the interest rate you will be charged is?

a. 1%

b. 2%

c. 4%

d. Minimum of $75

Answer C

If you are late with your payment on a HUD loan, a four percent (4%) late charge is implemented right away. All monthly payments have to be paid on a timely basis to avoid the penalty.

46. The most comprehensive ownership of real property known to the law is known as?

a. Fee simple absolute

b. Joint tenancy

c. Tenancy in common

d. Landlord

Answer A

Fee simple absolute is the ultimate form of holding a title in real estate. With this mode, the homeowner has absolute and unconditional ownership of the property.

47. Which type of tenancy is best for married people?

a. Joint tenancy

b. Tenancy in common

c. Tenancy in Entirety

d. Shared ownership

Answer C

For married couples, the best way to own a home is with Tenants by the Entirety. Under this tenancy, both the wife and husband are legally considered one individual. Tenancy in Entirety ensures that the property belongs to them as a single individual.

48. What protection does the Gramm-Leach-Bliley Act offer to consumers?

a. Refund of the down payment if the deal does not fall through

b. Right to complain to CFPB

c. Privacy

d. Lowest interest rates

Answer C

The Gramm-Leach-Bliley Act was passed to enhance the privacy of consumer finances by lenders and financial institutions.

49. The majority of fraud and deceptive practice violations in real estate are now managed by which agency?

a. CFPB

b. HUD

c. FHA

d. EOAC

Answer A

CFPB is now the ultimate government agency that legally enforces fraud and other violations in real estate financing. The overall goal is to protect consumers from charlatans and deceptive practices by lenders. CFPB carries enormous legal weight and is known for its harsh penalties.

50. Borrowers today can receive the Tool Booklet kit thanks to which law?

a. RESPA

b. Truth in lending

c. Homeowners Protection act

d. ECOA

Answer A

RESPA, or Real Estate Settlement Procedures Act, is also known as Regulation X. It ensures that all prospective home buyers who apply for a mortgage receive the Tool Booklet kit from the lender.

51. Which of the following is not a violation of the Fair Housing Act?

a. Disability

b. National origin

c. Religious beliefs

d. Advanced age

Answer D

The Fair Housing Act makes it illegal to discriminate on the basis of color, race, sex, religion, disability, national origin, and familial status.

52. What does the term 'encumbrance' mean in real estate?

a. Property does not belong to the seller

b. The property was obtained via deceptive practice

c. Property that is in foreclosure

d. The property has a claim on it but not by the owner

Answer D

Also referred to as an incumbrance, in the context of real estate, it means that there is a property claim made by someone other than the owner.

53. Which of the following is not an example of encumbrance?

a. Reverse mortgage

b. Lien

c. Easement

d. Encroachment

Answer A

Common types of encumbrances in real estate include deed restrictions, liens, encroachments, and easements. Some other types of encumbrances may also include liens that legally give another entity a right to use or claim your property.

54. What does 'trigger term' mean in real estate?

a. The lender appears to be deceptive

b. Referral bias for a loan

c. Disclosure during advertising

d. The home inspection may not be valid

Answer C

A triggering term is usually a phrase that legally mandates more disclosure, especially when it comes to advertising. Triggering terms have been defined by the Truth in Lending Act and help protect home buyers and borrowers from deceptive and predatory lending practices.

55. What is the right of rescission?

a. The right of lenders to cancel a loan

b. The right to foreclose on a home

c. The right of a seller to refuse a sale

d. The right of a borrower to cancel a loan within three days of the closing

Answer D

The right of rescission permits potential home buyers and borrowers to rescind or cancel a line of credit, a home equity loan, or refinance with a new bank/lender within three days of closing.

56. The primary goal of the Federal Trade Commission is to?

a. Ensure consumers know about low-interest rates

b. Deter unfair anti-competitive business practices

c. Ensure all lenders are licensed

d. Take legal action against fraud in real estate

Answer B

The FTC's mission is to protect the consumer from unfair or deceptive business practices. It also ensures that there are no biased methods of competition. It enforces compliance via research, advocacy, education, and law enforcement.

57. The components of a monthly mortgage payment are often referred to as?

a. PITI

b. DITTO

c. SEMI

d. ANTI

Answer A

PITI is an acronym that refers to principal, interest, taxes, and insurance. These four topics are the regular components of any loan/mortgage payment. PITI reflects the total monthly premiums and costs.

58. What is the additional 1/12 rule when dealing with mortgages?

a. You have to pay your monthly premiums each month for 12 months

b. You can miss one month of your mortgage payments

c. You can make an extra mortgage payment

d. One month of your mortgage payments has no interest

Answer C

By undertaking an extra mortgage payment each year, this can lower the total amount of the loan by a significant amount. The 1/12 maneuver is the easiest and least strenuous way to do this. For example, by paying $1500 each month on a $1,000 mortgage payment, the borrower will have paid at least six extra months' premium.

59. What is the 25% mortgage rule?

a. You should always make a 25% down payment

b. Your monthly debt should be 25% or less of your net income

c. You should only spend 25% of your monthly income on a mortgage

d. Never borrow more than 25% of the total value of the home

Answer B

The 25% model states the potential home buyer should have a total monthly debt of 25% or less of the post-tax income. For example, if the borrower makes $4,000 net every month, using his model, his debt should not be more than $4000 x 0.25 = $800 a month.

60. Your financial lender recently stated many people who buy homes are, in fact, considered 'house poor.' What does this term mean to you?

a. Homeowners buying homes beyond their means

b. Homeowners buying foreclosed homes

c. Homeowners are buying cheap homes

d. Buying a home in a poor neighborhood

Answer A

Frequently lenders and realtors use the expression "house broke" and "house poor." In simple words, this means that there are people buying homes beyond their financial means. For example, some people may buy a home with a pool but never consider the cost of pool maintenance; and eventually, the home costs become unmanageable.

61. What does a subordination letter usually mean?

a. The buyer has failed to pay his closing cost

b. The buyer has failed the credit check test

c. One debt has a priority over another debt when repaying a debtor

d. The lender has been deceptive with the loan disclosure

Answer C

When one debt takes priority over another debt, this is known as a subordination agreement. This legal document places priority on debts which is critical when one is facing foreclosure or bankruptcy.

62. The Truth in Lending Act was enacted in which year?

a. 1968

b. 1990

c. 2008

d. 2014

Answer A

The Truth in Lending Act (TILA) was enacted in 1968. This federal law was enacted to protect home buyers in their dealings with creditors and lenders and creditors.

63. Why is the Truth in Lending Act important?

a. It provides consumers with loan cost information

b. It allows the lender to refer clients to colleagues

c. It provides consumers with information about the lender

d. It allows the buyer to ask for everything in writing.

Answer A

The Truth in Lending Act (TILA) helps protect consumers against unfair and inaccurate billing and credit card practices. TILA mandates that banks and lenders provide consumers with loan cost information so that they can compare prices and shop around.

64. Which of the following is a conforming loan?

a. FHA

b. VA loan

c. USDA loan

d. Conventional loan

Answer D

Loans that meet Fannie Mae and Freddie Mac guidelines are said to be conforming loans. Conforming lenders underwrite and fund the loans and then sell them to investors like Freddie Mac and Fannie Mae.

65. In general, to get a conventional loan, what minimal credit score is necessary?

a. 550

b. 580

c. 620

d. 680

Answer C

Most lenders prefer that borrowers have good credit scores, more than 620. The higher the credit score, the greater the chance that the mortgage will be sealed, but for those with credit scores of less than 600, getting a mortgage may prove to be difficult. Most borrowers applying for a conventional mortgage have scores between 620-670.

66. What is one downside to an FHA loan?

a. It is only a short-term loan

b. It requires high credit scores

c. It requires mortgage insurance

d. It is only available to married people

Answer C

One of the biggest disadvantages of an FHA loan is the need to purchase private mortgage insurance, which can add significantly to the cost of the loan. Since FHA home loans are considered risky, borrowers usually need upfront mortgage insurance.

67. What is the minimum downpayment required for a conventional loan?

a. 3%

b. 7%

c. 10%

d. 20%

Answer A

The minimum down payment required for a conventional mortgage is 3%. However, borrowers with high debt-to-income ratios or low credit scores may be asked to put down a bigger down payment. For jumbo loans or a second home mortgage, there is usually a large down payment required.

68. For an FHA loan, who guarantees the loan?

a. The borrower

b. The FHA

c. The Banks

d. The USDA

Answer B

An FHA loan is guaranteed by the Federal Housing Administration. The FHA itself does not issue the loan but is willing to insure it. The money for the FHA loan is made available from banks and other financial institutions approved by the agency.

69. FICO scores are used to determine the borrowers?

a. History of Bankruptcy

b. Credit worthiness

c. Job stability

d. Disability

Answer B

Base FICO scores reveal to the bank or lender the credit worthiness of the borrower. All the lender is worried about is the ability of the borrower to repay the loan, whether it is a loan or a credit card bill.

70. The Act of passing the title of the home to another person is known as?

a. Conveyance

b. Transference

c. Distribution

d. Transportation

Answer A

When one transfers property to another party, this is known as conveyance. The term is widely used in property transactions when sellers and buyers transfer ownership of buildings, land, or homes. The act of conveyance is performed using a legal document that may be a lease, contract, or title.

71. In general, a mortgage pre-approval letter from a bank is valid for?

a. 14 days

b. 30 days

c. 60 days

d. 90 days

Answer D

Once a borrower has been pre-approved, the lender will provide a pre-approval letter; This is just an offer and not a firm commitment. The pre-approval letter is valid for 90 days.

72. What is meant by the term 'forced placed insurance?'

a. You have been forced to buy home insurance

b. The seller has already purchased home insurance for the buyer

c. The lender has purchased insurance for the property

d. You have been forced to sell the home because of a lack of insurance

Answer C

Sometimes the lender or bank will use Lender-placed (or Force-placed) insurance to cover a property that it owns. Lenders will do this to protect their assets when the borrower or homeowner fails to insure the property. For example, the owner may not insure a foreclosed home, and thus, the bank will insure the property to protect the asset.

73. What is the false statement about the power of Sale?

a. It may take 4-6 months

b. The lender is legally allowed to sell property

c. The former owner gets none of the profit

d. The lender does not get to keep the tile in the power of Sale.

Answer C

In Power of Sale, the lender sells the property; in foreclosure, the lender takes the title of the property. In Power of Sale, the former homeowner gets the excess profits from the Sale of the property; in foreclosure, the former homeowner gets nothing. The Power of Sale process takes around six months.

74. The CHARM booklet provides what type of information for the borrower?

a. General information on adjustable-rate mortgages

b. General information on fixed mortgages

c. General information on how to buy a home

d. Information on how to file for bankruptcy

Answer A

This "Consumer Handbook on Adjustable-Rate Mortgages" document explains what you need to know about adjustable-rate mortgages.

75. What does a 5-year ARM mean?

a. You pay no interest for the first five years

b. Your interest rates fluctuate for the first five years

c. Your interest rates remain fixed for the first five years

d. Your loan has a duration of 5 years.

Answer C

A 5-year ARM means that for the first five years, the interest rate is fixed. This rate will not change, irrespective of the economy. In most cases, with ARM, the initial rates are low, but once this period expires, the interest can go high, depending on the economy.

76. What was the main goal of the Dodd-Frank Act?

a. Educate consumers on the process of home buying

b. Prevent fraud and deceptive practices among lenders

c. Promote low-interest loans

d. Abolish the 20% down payment

Answer B

The Dodd-Frank Act led to a major reform on Wall street. The key goal of the act was to prevent fraud and deceptive practices among lenders. The act ensures that high-risk investments would be more transparent. The law also educates Americans on mortgage fraud and how to avoid being scammed.

77. The Consumer Financial Protection Bureau (CFPB) was established under which act?

a. ECOA

b. HUD

c. RESPA act

d. Dodd-Frank act

Answer D

The Consumer Financial Protection Bureau (CFPB) was created following the Dodd-Frank Act. The main purpose of the CFPB is to prevent predatory mortgage lending practices and educate consumers on mortgage terms.

78. Which rule restricts how banks can invest and limits speculative and proprietary trading

a. Volcker rule

b. Glass Steagall Act

c. Dodd-Frank Act

d. Truth in Lending Act

Answer A

The Volcker Rule limits how lenders and banks can invest, decrease speculative trading, and eliminate proprietary trading.

79. Under the Dodd-Frank Act, whistleblowers can receive how much of the reward?

a. 1-4%

b. 5-8 %

c. 10-30%

d. At least 50%

Answer C

The Dodd-Frank Act also led to the establishment of the whistleblower's program, under which they can receive anywhere from 10-30 percent of the proceeds following settlement.

80. The Home Ownership and Equity Protection Act was enacted three decades ago as an amendment to which act?

a. Truth in Lending Act

b. Real Estate Settlement Procedures Act

c. Consumer Protection Act

d. Dodd-Frank Wall Street Reform

Answer A

The Home Ownership and Equity Protection Act (HOEPA) was enacted nearly 30 years ago (1994) as an amendment to the Truth in Lending Act.

Practice Test 2

1. What is false about an adjustable rate mortgage?

a. Is a good long-term loan

b. Has interest rates that change

c. Initial monthly payments are low

d. It is considered to be a high-risk loan

Answer A

An adjustable-rate mortgage (ARM) is a loan with changing interest rates. ARMs usually start with low monthly premiums compared to fixed-rate mortgages, but in almost all cases, this changes with time. And as the interest rates change, so does the monthly premium. ARM loans are best for an individual who only wants to finance for a few years and then apply for other means of financing where the interest rates are fixed or predictable.

2. In general, how long do fixed-rate mortgages last?

a. Less than a year

b. Between two to ten years

c. Usually more than 20 years

d. As long as you want

Answer B

Fixed-rate mortgages usually have a duration between one to ten years. If the interest rates are low, most borrowers apply for the longest duration of the loan.

3. What is the most significant advantage of a fixed-rate mortgage?

a. It is a long-term loan

b. Monthly premiums remain the same

c. Interest rates are low

d. It can be canceled anytime without penalty

Answer B

The key advantage of a fixed-rate mortgage is that the monthly mortgage premiums remain the same for the duration of the loan. With a fixed-rate mortgage, the amount one pays towards the mortgage does not change for a specified number of years.

4. In general, the reason why is the loan-to-value ratio of importance?

a. It permits the potential buyer to get a bigger loan

b. It allows the lender to determine the risk of the loan

c. It permits the potential buyer to select his or her lender

d. It allows the lender to determine the size of the down payment

Answer B

The loan-to-value ratio is an essential assessment because it provides the lender with some information about the risk of the loan. If the loan-to-value ratio is high, then this is a red flag for a high-risk loan.

5. What does 70% loan-to-value mean?

a. The buyer will put down a 70% downpayment

b. The buyer will put down at least a 30% deposit

c. The lender will only give a loan of 30%

d. The lender will rescind the offer

Answer B

A 70% loan-to-value mortgage is a loan where the borrower puts down a deposit of at least 30% of the total property value which is being remortgaged or purchased. This means the borrower will need to obtain a mortgage of 70% from the bank or lender.

6. Lenders are usually required to give consumers the Good Faith Estimate documents at what time after closing?

a. Within three days

b. Within the first seven days

c. When the borrower asks for it

d. When the mortgage payments have started

Answer A

By law, the lender must provide the borrower with a good faith estimate document within three days of receiving the loan application. This document will include the total cost of the loan, including title change, taxes, administrative fees, and closing costs.

7. The Good Faith Estimate has been replaced by the?

a. Home loan toolkit

b. Loan estimate

c. Closing settlement document

d. Mortgage loan application document

Answer B

The good faith estimate was once the absolute guide to determine the costs of a loan, but the document has been replaced by the Loan Estimate.

8. During the initial stage of the loan application process, when disclosures have not been made, the lender can only charge the potential borrower with what fee?

a. Home inspection fee

b. Survey fee

c. Credit report fee

d. Consult fee

Answer C

During the initial stage of the loan application, the lender will only charge for the cost of doing a credit check. This may be done several times to ensure that the borrower's financial status has not altered. The cost of a credit check varies from $10 to $100.

9. What is the usual loan origination fee in the USA?

a. 0.5% to 1%

b. 3% to 5%

c. Depends on the property value

d. It depends on the lender

Answer A

An origination fee is usually between 0.5% to 1% of the loan amount. The lender charges this fee for processing the loan application. Sometimes the borrower may be able to negotiate this fee with the lender, but if the fee is waived, the borrower will end up paying high-interest rates over the life of the loan.

10. The loan estimate document will provide the borrower with information on all the below topics except?

a. Closing costs

b. Interest rate

c. Reverse mortgage

d. Costs to buy a home

Answer C

A loan estimate is a three-page document that is given to the borrower by the lender during the process of a loan application. Once the application is submitted, the lender has three days to give the borrower an estimate that details all the costs of purchasing a home, including the interest rates and closing costs. A loan estimate is not given when the borrower applies for a HELOC or a reverse mortgage.

11. In general, mortgage insurance is required when your down payment is?

a. Less than 3%

b. Less than 5%

c. Less than 10%

d. Less than 20%

Answer D

In general, across the country, mortgage loan insurance is required by lenders when the borrower makes a down payment of less than 20% of the home.

12. Regulation B is also known as the:

a. Equal Credit Opportunity Act

b. Truth in lending act

c. Fair housing act

d. Real Estate Settlement Procedures act

Answer A

Regulation B protects consumers and prohibits lenders from discriminating based on age, gender, ethnicity, nationality, or marital status.

13. What is a straw buyer?

a. Someone who only buys small homes

b. Someone who prefers a home that looks like a straw

c. A buyer who purchases property on behalf of someone else

d. A buyer who can only pay cash for the property

Answer C

A straw buyer is an individual who purchases a property in the name of another group, person, or entity which may or may not be part of a fraudulent plan.

14. The SAFE Act primarily refers to mortgage loans for which type of properties?

a. 1-4 non-owner occupied rentals

b. Individual condominiums

c. Motels

d. Schools

Answer B

The SAFE Act usually applies to residential properties and does not apply to real estate investments or commercial buildings.

15. How many hours of continuing education must MLOs complete each year?

a. 8

b.16

c. 20

d. 25

Answer A

All licensed mortgage loan officers are required to take a minimum of eight hours of continuing education every year. In addition, there may also be some specific state requirements to maintain the license.

16. RESPA does not cover which of the following loans?

a. Home equity lines of credit

b. Property improvement loans

c. Seller-financed mortgages

d. Loans on one to four-family residential properties

Answer C

RESPA, in general, applies to all "federally-related" real estate dealings that involve residential properties meant for one to four families. RESPA does not cover all loans, including mortgages for commercial properties, business investments, or agriculture.

17. An affiliate business arrangement is said to exist when a lender owns at least what percentage of a settlement service provider?

a. 1%

b. 5%

c. 25%

d. 50%

Answer A

An Affiliated Business Arrangement is said to exist when the individual in charge of financial services refers the customer to a real estate settlement service in which he or she has a direct financial interest. Even if the individual only has a 1% interest in the settlement business, a referral is not ethical and is considered a violation of RESPA.

18. How do you define appraisal?

a. Refers to the exact cost of a home

b. The cost of building a home

c. The market value of a home

d. Cost of a home following an inspection

Answer C

An appraisal is deemed to be a fair market valuation of an item/property, such as a business, real estate, antique, or collectible. The appraisal is usually done by an authorized professional.

19. After closing, when is the lender supposed to provide the initial escrow statement to the buyer?

a. ASAP

b. Within the first ten days

c. When the borrower asks for it

d. Within 45 days of the closing

Answer D

Once the closing is done, the initial escrow statement is usually given to the borrower at the time of the settlement or within 45 days of closing.

20. The Fair Credit Reporting Act (FRCA) is also known as Regulation?

a. A

b. C

c. Z

d. V

Answer D

Regulation V is a federal Act adopted by the Consumer Financial Protection Bureau. The Regulation ensures that all consumer data reported in a credit report will remain confidential and be protected at all times. The credit report also has to be accurate, as mandated by the Fair Credit Reporting Act.

21. What is true about a balloon mortgage?

a. It amortizes

b. The loan is paid back in a single sum

c. Comes with high-interest rates

d. It is usually a long-term loan

Answer B

A balloon mortgage is a type of property loan where the borrower makes none or very small monthly payments for a short period, usually about five to seven years. A balloon payment mortgage, unlike other mortgages, does not amortize over the duration of the loan. At maturity, the borrower has to repay the balance in one large sum.

22. One of the key reasons why many disclosure laws have been introduced in the lending business is to?

a. Make the consumer well-informed

b. To let the lender know that he or she is being monitored

c. Allow consumers to know the exact costs

d. Allows consumers to choose their service provider

Answer A

Prior to the 2007-2008 housing crisis, the mortgage industry was replete with fraud and deceptive practices. Since the Dodd-Frank Act, many other federal acts have been introduced in the world of loan service providers. The major aim of the disclosure laws is to make sure that the consumer is fully informed about the loan and lender practices.

23. An upfront mortgage insurance premium is often required for which type of loan?

a. USDA

b. VA

c. FHA

d. HUD

Answer C

Unlike many other loans, a residential single-family mortgage from the FHA does require an upfront mortgage insurance premium (MIP). Lenders must see proof of the MIP within ten calendar days of the mortgage closing, or the loan will be canceled.

24. Discrimination by lenders is prohibited by which law?

a. ECOA

b. RESPA

c. FHA

d. Dodd-Frank Act

Answer A

The federal civil rights law or the Equal Credit Opportunity Act (ECOA) is a federal government law that is a federal civil rights law that outlaws banks and private lenders from discriminating against borrowers for any reason other than the ability to repay back the loan. Specifically, the ECOA protects all borrowers from discrimination based on color, race, sex, religion, marital status, age, national origin, or reliance on public assistance.

25. An adverse action notice by the lender has to be submitted within how many days?

a. 7

b. 14

c. 21

d. 30

Answer D

In general, an adverse action notice by the lender must be submitted within 30 days.

26. What does the term 'escalation' mean in relation to a loan?

a. buyer can increase the offer in predetermined amounts whenever someone outbids

b. Buyer can shorten the time for loan closure

c. The seller can ask for rapid payments

d. The lender can perform a background check

Answer A

One of the clauses when making a lease or a real estate offer is the escalation clause. This clause makes it possible for the buyer to increase the offer in predetermined amounts whenever someone outbids the initial buyer. In simple terms, if there is a higher competing offer submitted by someone else, then the original buyer is allowed to increase his or her bid by a certain amount above the offer submitted.

27. What is the defeasance clause in a mortgage?

a. Substitute a collateral loan prepayment plan

b. Another name for fraud in loan servicing

c. Drop in interest rates

d. A home can go to foreclosure if one premium payment is missed

Answer A

Defeasance is a method of lowering the fees necessary when the borrower decides to prepay a fixed-rate commercial real estate loan. The defeasance clause permits the borrower to exchange another cash-flowing asset instead of paying cash to the lender. In simple terms, it is a penalty that involves the substitution of collateral.

28. What does the term escrow mean in real estate?

a. Paying off the mortgage sooner than expected

b. The lender holds the money until the background check is completed

c. It is the same as a security deposit

d. A legal arrangement where a third party holds the money

Answer D

Escrow is a legal maneuver where an independent third-party arrangement will hold property or money for a short term until a specified condition or payment has been fulfilled as per the purchase contract.

29. Once the buyer has paid off the remainder of his mortgage, how many days does the lender have to submit the satisfaction mortgage letter?

a. 10

b. 20

c. 30

d. 60

Answer D

In most states, once the borrower has paid off the mortgage, the lender has 60 days to submit the mortgage satisfaction letter.

30. National flood maps are usually provided by?

a. NASA

b. FDA

c. FEMA

d. Dept of Agriculture

Answer C

For potential home buyers who would like to know if the locality is at risk for flooding, one can obtain flood maps from FEMA. This agency provides flood maps for the entire country.

31. Who usually issues the Certificate of Reasonable value?

a. FHA

b. HUD

c. VA

d. Any lender

Answer C

The Certificate of Reasonable Value is issued by the Veterans Benefits Administration. This certificate is only provided after the home has been inspected by a VA-approved appraiser.

32. The Federal National Mortgage Association is also known as:

a. Freddie Mac

b. Fannie Mae

c. USDA

d. HUD

Both Freddie Mac and Fannie Mae were created by Congress so that they could play a critical role in the nation's financing of homes; Congress hoped that both would bring stability, transparency, and affordability to the mortgage industry. Both Freddie Mac and Fannie Mae do provide funds on reasonable terms to private lenders and banks across the nation. Unfortunately, both agencies functioned poorly, as was evident during the last housing crisis.

33. In general, loans for purchasing property in rural areas are issued by:

a. USDA

b. FDA

c. HUD

d. VA

Answer A

In general, for rural home buyers, USDA loans come with zero-down-payment mortgages. The USDA loans are only for those who are not able to get a traditional mortgage and are not wealthy.

34. What parameter does the income capitalization approach use to determine the market value of the property?

a. Size of the property

b. Location

c. Average offers on the property

d. Income generated

Answer D

The income capitalization approach, also known as the income approach, utilizes the amount of income generated from a property to determine its market value. The income-generated approach is typically utilized for commercial real estate, including apartment buildings, office buildings, and shopping centers.

35. Home Mortgage Disclosure Act is also known as Regulation:

a. C

b. N

c. X

d. Z

Answer A

The Home Mortgage Disclosure Act was enacted in 1975 by Congress. It was then implemented by the Federal Reserve Board and referred to as Regulation C.

36. The USDA loan requires a minimum credit score of?

a. 500

b. 640

c. 700

d. No credit score is required

Answer B

For those applying for a USDA loan, a minimum credit score of 640 is essential. However, the USDA does not only rely on credit scores to approve a loan, and some candidates with lower scores may be eligible for a USDA-backed mortgage.

37. What does the term 'exculpatory' mean in real estate?

a. Clause in the contract where one party limits the other party's liability

b. The borrower has financial liability

c. The lender has financial liability.

d. Both the lender and borrower are deemed financially liable

Answer A

The exculpatory clause in a lease, contract, or loan document is a clause whereby one party limits the other party's liability.

38. How does forbearance apply to your mortgage?

a. Pay the entire mortgage in full ahead of time

b. Intentionally reduce your mortgage payments

c. Put the home in foreclosure and avoid paying the mortgage

d. Ask the lender to pay your mortgage

Answer B

Forbearance is when the lender or mortgage servicer permits the borrower to reduce or pause the payments for a short period of time.

39. What is the minimum credit score required for Fannie Mae?

a. 600

b. 620

c. 650

d. 680

Answer B

To qualify for a loan from Fannie Mae, one has to have a credit score of at least 620. In fact, Fannie Mae prefers to give loans to people with high credit scores

40. What does a loan prospector evaluate?

a. Credit worthiness

b. Criminal history

c. Stable job

d. Experience with a home purchase

Answer A

The role of a Loan Prospector is to assess the credit worthiness of the borrower. After reviewing the borrower's financial and other data, he or she may make a recommendation for an FHA loan eligibility.

41. Which of the following is not true about a loan shark?

a. They are all licensed

b. They charge high-interest rates

c. They sometimes use threats when people do not pay back

d. They usually offer small loans

Answer A

In most cases, loan sharks are unscrupulous and unlicensed money lenders. They usually charge exorbitant interest rates and often use violence and threats to scare people who, unfortunately, are not able to repay the loan.

42. Which of the following is not typical of an amortized loan?

a. Credit card loan

b. Home Mortgage

c. Car loan

d. Student loan

Answer A

The majority of credit card loans are structured as non-amortizing loans. When obtaining a loan with a credit card, instead of paying back the principal on a scheduled payment plan, you only make the monthly minimum payments. Classic examples of amortized loans include car loans, conventional mortgages, and student loans.

43. What is a reverse mortgage?

a. Loan that is obtained without selling the home

b. A loan that is obtained by putting the home in escrow

c. A loan that is obtained by putting the home in foreclosure

d. A loan that comes with no interest

Answer A

A reverse mortgage is a loan that permits the borrower to obtain money from the home equity; there is usually no need to sell the home. But if the money is not repaid, it can quickly lead to repossession by the lender.

44. The Home Mortgage Disclosure Act is also known as Regulation?

a. B

b. C

c. N

d. Z

Answer B

The Home Mortgage Disclosure Act was enacted in 1975 by Congress and later implemented by the Federal Reserve Board is known as Regulation C.

45. If you are going to buy a home with a USDA loan, how much downpayment is necessary?

a. None

b. 3%

c. 10%

d. Minimum of 20%

Answer A

Unlike most other loans, a USDA loan does not require any down payment. However, you still need a minimum credit score of 580 to be eligible for the loan. The USDA loan is for the purchase of property in rural areas.

46. If you are late with your monthly premium on a HUD loan, the interest rate you will be charged is?

a. 1%

b. 2%

c. 4%

d. Minimum of $75

Answer C

If you are late with your payment on a HUD loan, a four percent (4%) late charge is implemented right away. All monthly payments have to be paid on a timely basis to avoid the penalty.

47. The most comprehensive ownership of real property known to the law is known as?

a. Fee simple absolute

b. Joint tenancy

c. Tenancy in common

d. Landlord

Answer A

Fee simple absolute is the ultimate form of holding a title in real estate. With this mode, the homeowner has absolute and unconditional ownership of the property.

48. Which type of tenancy is best for married people?

a. Joint tenancy

b. Tenancy in common

c. Tenancy in Entirety

d. Shared ownership

Answer C

For married couples, the best way to own a home is with Tenants by the Entirety. Under this tenancy, both the wife and husband are legally considered one individual. Tenancy in Entirety ensures that the property belongs to them as a single individual.

49. What protection does the Gramm-Leach-Bliley Act offer to consumers?

a. Refund of the down payment if the deal does not fall through

b. Right to complain to CFPB

c. Privacy

d. Lowest interest rates

Answer C

The Gramm-Leach-Bliley Act was passed to enhance the privacy of consumer finances by lenders and financial institutions.

50. The majority of fraud and deceptive practice violations in real estate are now managed by which agency?

a. CFPB

b. HUD

c. FHA

d. EOAC

Answer A

CFPB is now the ultimate government agency that legally enforces fraud and other violations in real estate financing. The overall goal is to protect consumers from charlatans and deceptive practices by lenders. CFPB carries enormous legal weight and is known for its harsh penalties.

51. Borrowers today can receive the Tool Booklet kit thanks to which law?

a. RESPA

b. Truth in lending

c. Homeowners Protection act

d. ECOA

Answer A

RESPA, or Real Estate Settlement Procedures Act, is also known as Regulation X. It ensures that all prospective home buyers who apply for a mortgage receive the Tool Booklet kit from the lender.

52. Which of the following is not a violation of the Fair Housing Act?

a. Disability

b. National origin

c. Religious beliefs

d. Advanced age

Answer D

The Fair Housing Act makes it illegal to discriminate on the basis of color, race, sex, religion, disability, national origin, and familial status.

53. What does the term 'encumbrance' mean in real estate?

a. Property does not belong to the seller

b. The property was obtained via deceptive practice

c. Property that is in foreclosure

d. The property has a claim on it but not by the owner

Answer D

Also referred to as an incumbrance, in the context of real estate, it means that there is a property claim made by someone other than the owner.

54. Which of the following is not an example of encumbrance?

a. Reverse mortgage

b. Lien

c. Easement

d. Encroachment

Answer A

Common types of encumbrances in real estate include deed restrictions, liens, encroachments, and easements. Some other types of encumbrances may also include liens that legally give another entity a right to use or claim your property.

55. What does 'trigger term' mean in real estate?

a. The lender appears to be deceptive

b. Referral bias for a loan

c. Disclosure during advertising

d. The home inspection may not be valid

Answer C

A triggering term is usually a phrase that legally mandates more disclosure, especially when it comes to advertising. Triggering terms have been defined by the Truth in Lending Act and help protect home buyers and borrowers from deceptive and predatory lending practices.

56. What is the right of rescission?

a. The right of lenders to cancel a loan

b. The right to foreclose on a home

c. The right of a seller to refuse a sale

d. The right of a borrower to cancel a loan within three days of the closing

Answer D

The right of rescission permits potential home buyers and borrowers to rescind or cancel a line of credit, a home equity loan, or refinance with a new bank/lender within three days of closing.

57. The primary goal of the Federal Trade Commission is to?

a. Ensure consumers know about low-interest rates

b. Deter unfair anti-competitive business practices

c. Ensure all lenders are licensed

d. Take legal action against fraud in real estate

Answer B

The FTC's mission is to protect the consumer from unfair or deceptive business practices. It also ensures that there are no biased methods of competition. It enforces compliance via research, advocacy, education, and law enforcement.

58. The components of a monthly mortgage payment are often referred to as?

a. PITI

b. DITTO

c. SEMI

d. ANTI

Answer A

PITI is an acronym that refers to principal, interest, taxes, and insurance. These four topics are the regular components of any loan/mortgage payment. PITI reflects the total monthly premiums and costs.

59. What is the additional 1/12 rule when dealing with mortgages?

a. You have to pay your monthly premiums each month for 12 months

b. You can miss one month of your mortgage payments

c. You can make an extra mortgage payment

d. One month of your mortgage payments has no interest

Answer C

By undertaking an extra mortgage payment each year, this can lower the total amount of the loan by a significant amount. The 1/12 maneuver is the easiest and least strenuous way to do this. For example, by paying $1500 each month on a $1,000 mortgage payment, the borrower will have paid at least six extra months' premium.

60. What is the 25% mortgage rule?

a. You should always make a 25% down payment

b. Your monthly debt should be 25% or less of your net income

c. You should only spend 25% of your monthly income on a mortgage

d. Never borrow more than 25% of the total value of the home

Answer B

The 25% model states the potential home buyer should have a total monthly debt of 25% or less of the post-tax income. For example, if the borrower makes $4,000 net every month, using his model, his debt should not be more than $4000 x 0.25 = $800 a month.

61. Your financial lender recently stated many people who buy homes are, in fact, considered 'house poor.' What does this term mean to you?

a. Homeowners buying homes beyond their means

b. Homeowners buying foreclosed homes

c. Homeowners are buying cheap homes

d. Buying a home in a poor neighborhood

Answer A

Frequently lenders and realtors use the expression "house broke" and "house poor." In simple words, this means that there are people buying homes beyond their financial means. For example, some people may buy a home with a pool but never consider the cost of pool maintenance; and eventually, the home costs become unmanageable.

62. What does a subordination letter usually mean?

a. The buyer has failed to pay his closing cost

b. The buyer has failed the credit check test

c. One debt has a priority over another debt when repaying a debtor

d. The lender has been deceptive with the loan disclosure

Answer C

When one debt takes priority over another debt, this is known as a subordination agreement. This legal document places priority on debts which is critical when one is facing foreclosure or bankruptcy.

63. The Truth in Lending Act was enacted in which year?

a. 1968

b. 1990

c. 2008

d. 2014

Answer A

The Truth in Lending Act (TILA) was enacted in 1968. This federal law was enacted to protect home buyers in their dealings with creditors and lenders and creditors.

64. Why is the Truth in Lending Act important?

a. It provides consumers with loan cost information

b. It allows the lender to refer clients to colleagues

c. It provides consumers with information about the lender

d. It allows the buyer to ask for everything in writing.

·Answer A

The Truth in Lending Act (TILA) helps protect consumers against unfair and inaccurate billing and credit card practices. TILA mandates that banks and lenders provide consumers with loan cost information so that they can compare prices and shop around.

65. Which of the following is a conforming loan?

a. FHA

b. VA loan

c. USDA loan

d. Conventional loan

Answer D

Loans that meet Fannie Mae and Freddie Mac guidelines are said to be conforming loans. Conforming lenders underwrite and fund the loans and then sell them to investors like Freddie Mac and Fannie Mae.

66. In general, to get a conventional loan, what minimal credit score is necessary?

a. 550

b. 580

c. 620

d. 680

Answer C

Most lenders prefer that borrowers have good credit scores, more than 620. The higher the credit score, the greater the chance that the mortgage will be sealed, but for those with credit scores of less than 600, getting a mortgage may prove to be difficult. Most borrowers applying for a conventional mortgage have scores between 620-670.

67. What is one downside to an FHA loan?

a. It is only a short-term loan

b. It requires high credit scores

c. It requires mortgage insurance

d. It is only available to married people

Answer C

One of the biggest disadvantages of an FHA loan is the need to purchase private mortgage insurance, which can add significantly to the cost of the loan. Since FHA home loans are considered risky, borrowers usually need upfront mortgage insurance.

68. What is the minimum downpayment required for a conventional loan?

a. 3%

b. 7%

c. 10%

d. 20%

Answer A

The minimum down payment required for a conventional mortgage is 3%. However, borrowers with high debt-to-income ratios or low credit scores may be asked to put down a bigger down payment. For jumbo loans or a second home mortgage, there is usually a large down payment required.

69. For an FHA loan, who guarantees the loan?

a. The borrower

b. The FHA

c. The Banks

d. The USDA

Answer B

An FHA loan is guaranteed by the Federal Housing Administration. The FHA itself does not issue the loan but is willing to insure it. The money for the FHA loan is made available from banks and other financial institutions approved by the agency.

70. FICO scores are used to determine the borrowers?

a. History of Bankruptcy

b. Credit worthiness

c. Job stability

d. Disability

Answer B

Base FICO scores reveal to the bank or lender the credit worthiness of the borrower. All the lender is worried about is the ability of the borrower to repay the loan, whether it is a loan or a credit card bill.

71. The Act of passing the title of the home to another person is known as?

a. Conveyance

b. Transference

c. Distribution

d. Transportation

Answer A

When one transfers property to another party, this is known as conveyance. The term is widely used in property transactions when sellers and buyers transfer ownership of buildings, land, or homes. The act of conveyance is performed using a legal document that may be a lease, contract, or title.

72. In general, a mortgage pre-approval letter from a bank is valid for?

a. 14 days

b. 30 days

c. 60 days

d. 90 days

Answer D

Once a borrower has been pre-approved, the lender will provide a pre-approval letter; This is just an offer and not a firm commitment. The pre-approval letter is valid for 90 days.

73. What is meant by the term 'forced placed insurance?'

a. You have been forced to buy home insurance

b. The seller has already purchased home insurance for the buyer

c. The lender has purchased insurance for the property

d. You have been forced to sell the home because of a lack of insurance

Answer C

Sometimes the lender or bank will use Lender-placed (or Force-placed) insurance to cover a property that it owns. Lenders will do this to protect their assets when the borrower or homeowner fails to insure the property. For example, the owner may not insure a foreclosed home, and thus, the bank will insure the property to protect the asset.

74. What is the false statement about the power of Sale?

a. It may take 4-6 months

b. The lender is legally allowed to sell property

c. The former owner gets none of the profit

d. The lender does not get to keep the tile in the power of Sale.

Answer C

In Power of Sale, the lender sells the property; in foreclosure, the lender takes the title of the property. In Power of Sale, the former homeowner gets the excess profits from the Sale of the property; in foreclosure, the former homeowner gets nothing. The Power of Sale process takes around six months.

75. The CHARM booklet provides what type of information for the borrower?

a. General information on adjustable-rate mortgages

b. General information on fixed mortgages

c. General information on how to buy a home

d. Information on how to file for bankruptcy

Answer A

This "Consumer Handbook on Adjustable-Rate Mortgages" document explains what you need to know about adjustable-rate mortgages.

76. What does a 5-year ARM mean?

a. You pay no interest for the first five years

b. Your interest rates fluctuate for the first five years

c. Your interest rates remain fixed for the first five years

d. Your loan has a duration of 5 years.

Answer C

A 5-year ARM means that for the first five years, the interest rate is fixed. This rate will not change, irrespective of the economy. In most cases, with ARM, the initial rates are low, but once this period expires, the interest can go high, depending on the economy.

77. What was the main goal of the Dodd-Frank Act?

a. Educate consumers on the process of home buying

b. Prevent fraud and deceptive practices among lenders

c. Promote low-interest loans

d. Abolish the 20% down payment

Answer B

The Dodd-Frank Act led to a major reform on Wall street. The key goal of the act was to prevent fraud and deceptive practices among lenders. The act ensures that high-risk investments would be more transparent. The law also educates Americans on mortgage fraud and how to avoid being scammed.

78. The Consumer Financial Protection Bureau (CFPB) was established under which

act?

a. ECOA

b. HUD

c. RESPA act

d. Dodd-Frank act

Answer D

The Consumer Financial Protection Bureau (CFPB) was created following the Dodd-Frank Act. The main purpose of the CFPB is to prevent predatory mortgage lending practices and educate consumers on mortgage terms.

79. Which rule restricts how banks can invest and limits speculative and proprietary trading

a. Volcker rule

b. Glass Steagall Act

c. Dodd-Frank Act

d. Truth in Lending Act

Answer A

The Volcker Rule limits how lenders and banks can invest, decrease speculative trading, and eliminate proprietary trading.

80. Under the Dodd-Frank Act, whistleblowers can receive how much of the reward?

a. 1-4%

b. 5-8 %

c. 10-30%

d. At least 50%

Answer C

The Dodd-Frank Act also led to the establishment of the whistleblower's program, under which they can receive anywhere from 10-30 percent of the proceeds following settlement.

81. The Home Ownership and Equity Protection Act was enacted three decades ago as an amendment to which act?

a. Truth in Lending Act

b. Real Estate Settlement Procedures Act

c. Consumer Protection Act

d. Dodd-Frank Wall Street Reform

Answer A

The Home Ownership and Equity Protection Act (HOEPA) was enacted nearly 30 years ago (1994) as an amendment to the Truth in Lending Act.

Practice Test 3

1. The RESPA Statute covers mortgage loans on what types of property?

a. Residential properties 1-4 units

b. Commercial property

c. Rental property transaction

d. All cash sale

Answer A

In general, RESPA covers loans that have been secured with a mortgage on personal property that includes one-to-four-family residential units.

2. What is dual tracking?

a. When a borrower has applied for two simultaneous loans

b. When the lender pursues foreclosure while also assisting the borrower in mitigating foreclosure

c. When the lender tracks both the primary and secondary loans

d. When the borrower is trying to repay two loans at the same time

Answer B

Dual tracking is when a mortgage servicer does two things simultaneously; they pursue foreclosure on a home while at the same time assisting the homeowner with a loan modification or other financial alternative.

3. What does it mean if your home is in loss mitigation?

a. You are not able to find a buyer

b. The home value is severely reduced

c. Motions the loan services take to prevent foreclosure

d. You have lowered your risk of foreclosure

Answer C

Loss mitigation refers to the process whereby mortgage servicer providers work with the loan borrower to avoid or lower the risk of foreclosure.

4. Which of the following is not a 'cap' on an ARM?

a. Initial interest rate

b. Period of time

c. Interest increases every year

d. Lifetime rate

Answer C

With an adjustable-rate mortgage, the initial interest rate remains fixed for a specified duration of time, for example, in the case of a 5/1 ARM. After this time, the process resets regularly depending on the current interest rates every year (i.e., the "1" in the 5/1). ARMs usually have a lifetime rate cap that restricts how much interest will increase over the lifespan of the mortgage.

5. What does the number '5' mean in an ARM cap of 2 1 5?

a. The interest rate cannot increase or decrease more than 5% over the lifetime of the loan

b. The total duration of the loan is five years

c. The initial interest rate starts at five years

d. The interest rate will fall to zero at the end of 5 years

Answer A

In an ARM with a 2/1/5 cap structure, this means that the loan can fall or increase by 2% during the first adjustment and up to 1% with every periodic adjustment after that- which is usually a year. Finally, the interest rate can't decrease or increase greater than 5% below or above the initial rate over the entire lifetime of your home loan.

6. A real estate agreement requires the borrower to pay the remaining balance of the loan immediately after the sale or transfer of ownership of a property. This is known as?

a. Alienation clause

b. Acceleration clause

c. Exculpatory clause

d. Defeasance clause

Answer A

"Alienation" means that there is a transfer of property rights and ownership. The alienation clause states that the borrower must pay the full mortgage upon transfer of the property.

7. In general, what is the lowest credit score you need to purchase a home in the USA?

a. 550

b. 580

c. 600

d. 620

Answer D

Generally speaking, borrowers for conventional loans need to have a decent credit score; lenders usually require a score of at least 620 to be eligible for a home mortgage. This is the minimum credit score for conventional loans. But it is still possible to obtain a loan with a low credit score if the borrower has a large down payment, a great job, a low debt-to-income ratio, etc.

8. When a contract states that one party cannot sue another party for any damage related to the contract, this is known as the?

a. Exculpatory clause

b. Integration clause

c. Acceleration clause

d. Alienation clause

Answer A

An exculpatory clause is sometimes included in the contract; it usually prevents one party from suing the other party for any damages related to the contract. Exculpatory clauses are used frequently when consumers purchase airline tickets or visit amusement centers-where cancellations of flights and rides are not uncommon.

9. In general, how many loans can a consumer have with Fannie Mae?

a. One only

b. 2

c. 4-10

d. Unlimited

Answer C

Fannie Mae allows borrowers to finance 4-10 mortgages at the same time. However, this also requires an excellent credit score and a very low debt-to-income ratio.

10. How many credit scores does Fannie Mae require for each borrower?

a. 1

b. 2

c. 4

d. 5

Answer B

Fannie Mae usually obtains a minimum of two credit scores for each borrower. When two credit scores are obtained, the one with the lower score is usually selected.

11. What is the minimum credit score required for a Fannie Mae Loan?

a. 580

b. 600

c. 620

d. 680

Answer C

One of the criteria for a Fannie Mae loan is that the borrower must have a minimum qualifying credit score of 620, but even with this relatively low score, many borrowers do not qualify in getting a loan. The reason is that many borrowers today have very high debt-to-income ratios.

12. What credit score model is used by most lenders?

a. FICO

b. Vantage score

c. Infosys

d. Das Kapital

Answer A

Today, most lenders in the USA use FICO Scores to determine the applicant's credit status. The FICO score gives the lender more insight into the borrower's credit risk.

13. In real estate, what does 'Alt A' stand for?

a. American loan title agreement

b. American land title association

c. American loan time agreement

d. American land title award

Answer B

The American Land Title Association (ALTA) plays a critical role in the residential title insurance industry. The history of the ownership of the property can be traced.

14. What is a key feature of an 'Alt A' loan?

a. It does not require a credit history

b. It is relatively easy to obtain

c. It is a type of conforming loan

d. Available with minimal documentation

Answer D

An Alt-A loan is one that requires little or no documentation to obtain a mortgage. These loans are not easy to get. Loans that permit 100% financing of the property also can be categorized as Alt-a.

15. A method that focuses on spreading out loan payments over time is known as?

a. Amortization

b. Depreciation

c. Accretion

d. Repudiation

Answer A

When there is a fixed payment plan for the mortgage to be paid back over time, this is known as amortization. The loan is usually paid off at the end of the payment schedule.

16. An increase in the principal balance as a result of failure to cover the interest on the loan is known as?

a. Amortization

b. Negative amortization

c. Accretion

d. Depreciation

Answer B

When a borrower pays less than the monthly premium owed, the principal amount on the loan tends to increase because the loan payments are insufficient. This is known as negative amortization.

17. What is a senior mortgage?

a. Same as a junior mortgage

b. The primary mortgage

c. The secondary mortgage

d. The last mortgage

Answer B

The senior mortgage is often referred to as the primary mortgage. A second mortgage is referred to as a junior mortgage and may be offered in combination with the primary mortgage.

18. What is a junior mortgage?

a. A home loan made in addition to the primary mortgage

b. A primary home loan

c. A home loan that is less than $100K

d. A home loan that is available for a second home

Answer A

A junior mortgage refers to a second mortgage that is granted in conjunction with the approval of an effective primary or prior mortgage. The primary mortgage is referred to as a senior mortgage. A junior mortgage can also be a third, fourth, or fifth mortgage granted after the security of a senior mortgage.

19. A mortgage where the borrower makes no or little monthly payments but pays the entire principal at maturity is known as a?

a. Fixed-rate mortgage

b. Balloon Mortgage

c. Convertible mortgage

d. Hybrid mortgage

Answer B

In real estate, a balloon mortgage usually may have no or very low monthly payments, but at the end, the borrower will be asked to pay a lump sum to pay off the mortgage; this is typical of a balloon mortgage.

20. An abusive practice pushed by the lender where a loan is refinanced without any tangible net benefit to the borrower is known as?

a. Loan flipping

b. Loan packing

c. Loan fixing

d. Equity skimming

Answer A

Loan flipping is a predatory lending practice that was common in the past. With loan flipping, the lenders usually convenience the borrower to refinance their property by accepting a new long-term loan at higher costs but with no potential benefit.

21. A creditor must respond to a mortgage service payoff statement request within how many days?

a. 24 hours

b. Two days

c. Seven days

d. 14 days

Answer C

By law, the mortgage service provider must get in touch with the borrower within seven days, excluding official public holidays and weekends.

22. In 2008, which government agency took over control of Fannie Mae and Freddie Mac?

a. FHA

b. NHA

c. RESPA

d. FHFA

Answer D

After the housing crisis in 2008, in September of the same year, the Federal Housing Finance Agency (FHFA) stated that it was taking over both Fannie Mae (Federal National Mortgage Association) and Freddie Mac (Federal Home Loan Mortgage Corporation).

23. Who is said to be the most responsible for the 2008 mortgage crisis?

a. The borrowers

b. The lenders

c. The government

d. The home builders

Answer B

Most of the blame for the 2008 housing crisis was on the lenders and mortgage originators. The reason is that these people had deceptive and fraudulent lending practices that led to loans to individuals with poor credit.

24. What is form 442?

a. An appraisal update and completion report

b. Renewal form for the primary mortgagee

c. Agreed action and personal development plan

d. Form to inspect a residential property

Answer A

Form 442 was created to document an update of an appraisal and to determine if a new appraisal was necessary.

25. What is the appraisal recertification form called?

a. Form 442

b. Form 1030

c. Form 100

d. Form S

Answer A

Form 442 was created to document an update of an appraisal and to determine if a new appraisal was necessary.

26. A borrower's payment history on previous mortgages and rent must be verified for how long when evaluating for a loan?

a. Three months

b. Six months

c. Nine months

d. Twelve months

Answer D

In general, lenders must verify the applicant's home payment history including rentals for the most recent year (or 12 months) when considering a loan.

27. You can't ask how many children a borrower has to avoid discrimination against people with families, so what question(s) would you ask?

a. Do you have any dependents?

b. Do you have people under 18 living at home

c. How big is your family?

d. All of the above

Answer D

All the above questions can be asked instead of asking directly how many children the borrower has.

28. What entity or agency is responsible for enforcing the Equal Credit Opportunity Act?

a. HUD

b. FDA

c. VA

d. CFPB

Answer D

CFPB has established an Office of Fair Lending and Equal Opportunity that is directly responsible for enforcing ECOa.

29. When the statement on the mortgage contract states that the property title will be transferred to the borrower when the payment conditions are satisfied, this is known as

what clause?

a. Defeasance

b. Yield maintenance

c. Trigger clause

d. Prepayment

Answer A

A defeasance clause is a term within a mortgage contract that states the property's title will be transferred to the borrower (mortgagor) when he or she satisfies the payment conditions from the lender (mortgagee).

30. When a mortgage agreement establishes a priority order of debt payments from a note holder by making one debt superior, this is known as?

a. Subordination clause

b. Defeasance clause

c. Yield maintenance

d. Trigger clause

Answer A

Subordination is a process of ranking home loans (e.g., home equity loan, home mortgage, HELOC, etc.) by order of importance. For example, when you have a home mortgage and also a home equity line of credit, you are dealing with two loans. While both mortgages are secured by the home equity the subordination clause will state the priority on which loan the borrower must pay first.

31. When a buyer states in the contract that he is willing to increase upon the agreed-upon price of the home, this is known as?

a. Subordination clause

b. Escalation clause

c. Defeasance clause

d. Appreciation clause

Answer B

An escalator clause is a provision in the contract that permits an increase in agreed-upon price, wages, or rent under certain conditions.

32. What are the maximum seller concessions on a conventional loan if the downpayment is less than 10%?

a. 1%

b. 3%

c. 5%

d. 7%

Answer B

The concession limit for conventional loans depends on how much the borrower is going to be putting down. If the down payment is less than 10%, the seller will usually contribute up to 3%. If the down payment is between 10% to 25%, the seller may contribute up to 6%. If the down payment is greater than 25%, the seller can contribute up to 9%.

33. What is the maximum seller concession on FHA loans?

a. 1%

b. 2%

c. 4%

d. 6%

Answer D

FHA seller concessions are capped at 6% of the sales price or 6% of the appraised value, whichever is less.

34. What are the maximum seller concessions on a VA loan?

a. 1%

b. 2%

c. 4%

d. 6%

Answer C

On VA loans, the maximum seller concessions cannot exceed more than 4% of the lesser of the home purchase price.

35. What are the maximum seller concessions on a USDA loan?

a. 1%

b. 2%

c. 4%

d. 6%

Answer D

USDA loan guidelines recommend that the seller may contribute up to 6% of the sales price toward the buyer's reasonable closing costs.

36. What is the maximum debt-to-income ratio when applying for a USDA loan?

a. 25% or less

b. 30% or less

c. 41% or less

d. 50% or less

Answer C

For people applying for a USDA loan, the individual must have Proof of citizenship (or legal permanent residency), a debt-to-income ratio of 41% or less, and a minimum credit score of around 620.

37. What does it mean when a certificate of lis pendens is registered on the property title?

a. Owner has been sued, but there is no judgment

b. The owner has been sued and found to be guilty

c. The owner does not own the property anymore

d. The owner is about to file for bankruptcy

Answer A

When there is a certificate of lis pendens registered on a property title, this usually indicates that there is litigation involved; most likely the home or property owner has been sued but judgment is pending.

38. What is it called when a notice is filed in public records indicating that there is a legal proceeding pending asserting a claim against the title?

a. Lien

b. Lis pendens

c. Reverse lien

d. Pending litigation

Answer B

When there is a certificate of lis pendens registered on a property title, this usually indicates that the property owner has been sued, but as of now, there is no judgment.

39. When there is a court ruling against a borrower who is in default on a secured loan, this is known as?

a. Deficiency judgment

b. Defense deficiency

c. Property is foreclosed

d. Final judgment

Answer A

A Deficiency judgment occurs when money is awarded to lenders/creditors when assets securing a loan do not cover the debt owed by the borrower.

40. In general, a deficiency judgment will stay on the credit report for how long?

a. Two years

b. Five years

c. Seven years

d. Ten years

Answer C

A deficiency judgment usually remains on the borrower's credit report for seven years. This is a negative judgment that makes it difficult to obtain all other types of loans.

41. The home equity conversion mortgage is a reverse mortgage offered by which agency?

a. FHA

b. NHA

c. VA

d. USDA

Answer A

A Home equity mortgage is not issued by the government; It is a loan issued by a mortgage lender but is insured by the Federal Housing Administration, which is part of HUD.

42. What is the most common type of reverse mortgage offered in real estate?

a. HECM

b. HELOC

c. Single purpose reverse mortgage

d. Proprietary reverse mortgage not issued by the FHA

Answer A

Reverse mortgages are relatively common; homeowners apply for a Home Equity Conversion Mortgage (HECM) which is the most common reverse mortgage on the market. HECM is primarily insured by the Federal Housing Administration (FHA), which is a subsidiary of HUD.

43. To be eligible for a home equity conversion mortgage, the individual has to be at least what age?

a. 18

b. 45

c. 62

d. 70

Answer C

The most common type of reverse mortgage, the Home Equity Conversion Mortgage (HECM), is only for homeowners who are age 62 or older.

44. What is not a major disadvantage of a reverse mortgage?

a. Loss of home equity

b. Long-term costs

c. Variable interest rates

d. Ability to deduct tax

Answer D

Although a reverse mortgage enables the homeowner to tap into a large sum of money, this particular mortgage has several negatives. The interest paid on the reverse mortgage is not tax deductible until the loan is completely paid off.

45. If the home value is $200,000, the average fee for a reverse mortgage is?

a. 1% of the property value

b. 2% of the property value

c. A fixed rate of $2000

d. 5% of the property value

Answer B

The usual fee for a reverse mortgage is 2% of the first $200,000 of the property's value and 1% of the amount over $200,000. There is a maximum of $6,000 origination fee. A lender may charge a HECM origination fee of up to $2,500 if your home is valued at less than $125,000.

46. Which Act requires that state licensing and federal registration be accomplished through the Nationwide Mortgage Licensing System and Registry?

a. Safe Act

b. RESPA

c. Federal Housing Act

d. National Housing Act

Answer A

The SAFE Act made it mandatory that state licensing and federal registration be completed via the Nationwide Mortgage Licensing System and Registry. All this can be done online on its website

47. What does the SAFE Act stand for?

a. Safe and Fast Enforcement for Mortgage Licensing act

b. Safe and Forever Encouragement of the Mortgage Licensing act

c. Secure and Fast Expedition of the Mortgage licensing act

d. Secure and Fair Enforcement for Mortgage Licensing Act

Answer D

The SAFE Mortgage Licensing Act was created to improve consumer protection and decrease fraud by encouraging all US states to establish minimum standards for the registration and licensing of state-licensed mortgage loan originators.

48. What does FACTA stand for?

a. Federal Association Commission for Trade associations

b. Fair and Accurate Credit Transaction Act

c. Federal American Consumer Trade Complaints

d. Foreign Account Certification Trade Agreement

Answer B

FACTA stands for the Fair and Accurate Credit Transaction Act. Whether you have been a victim of fraud or have a dispute with a transaction, FACTA will provide the consumer with the relevant details.

49. Who enforces the Fair and Accurate Credit Transaction Act?

a. NRA

b. CFPB

c. FTC

d. DEA

Answer C

When there is non-compliance with FACTA regarding financial transactions involving credit cards, the FTC will conduct a compliance audit of FACTA. There are major penalties for any major errors.

50. Who enforces ECOA?

a. RESPA

b. CFPB

c. HUD

d. FTC

Answer B

The Consumer Financial Protection Bureau oversees and enforces ECOA violations. These regulations, known as Regulation B, provide the procedural and substantive framework for fair and honest lending practices.

51. If an individual is guilty of violating ECOA, what is the monetary penalty?

a. $2,500

b. $5,000

c. $10,000

d. $50,000

Answer C

If a lender is guilty of violating any part of ECOA, it can be sued in court for actual damages, including punitive damages of up to $10,000 for individual lawsuits and $500,000 or 1% of the creditor's net worth for class-action lawsuits.

52. The Truth in Lending Act does not apply to?

a. Auto loans

b. Home mortgages

c. Credit cards

d. Agriculture businesses

Answer D

The Truth in Lending Act applies to many types of financial transactions including the different types of consumer credit, such as auto loans, mortgages, and credit cards. The Truth in Lending Act, however, does not apply to many businesses, public utilities, certain student loans and home fuel budget loans.

53. The Truth in Lending Act has been replaced by the following:

a. Home Ownership and Equity Protection Act

b. RESPA

c. National Housing Act

d. ECOA

Answer A

The Home Ownership and Equity Protection Act of 1994 (HOEPA) amended the TILA. The law imposed new disclosure requirements and substantive limitations on certain closed-end mortgage loans bearing fees or rates above a specified amount or percentage.

54. Which of the following is not covered by the Truth in Lending Act?

a. Credit card loans

b. Home loans

c. Student loans

d. Car loans

Answer C

The TILA does not cover loans over $25K given for purposes other than housing, student loans, and business loans. The TILA only protects consumer credit and loans.

55. Once a loan application is made, how long does the lender have to disclose the Loan Estimate?

a. 24 hours

b. Three days

c. Five days

d. Seven days

Answer B

The mortgage officer or agency must provide the Loan Estimate to applicants within three business days after a loan application has been submitted. The second part; referred to as the Closing Disclosure, is meant to provide disclosures to potential applicants about all the different costs associated with a loan.

56. A second mortgage, usually a home equity loan, created at the same time as the main mortgage is also known as?

a. Piggyback loan

b. Junior mortgage

c. Secondary loan

d. Tertiary loan

Answer A

When a borrower obtains a second mortgage like a home equity line of credit (HELOC) or a home equity loan at the same time as obtaining the primary mortgage, this is known as a piggyback loan. The piggyback loan permits borrowers who only have a small down payment to save money; because with the additional funds the borrower can now qualify for the main mortgage without having to purchase private mortgage insurance.

57. The Real Estate Settlement Procedures Act is overseen by which agency?

a. HUD

b. FTC

c. ECOA

d. CFPB

Answer D

RESPA is under the oversight and enforcement of the CFPB and is oriented toward consumer protection enforcement.

58. The sequence of historical transfers of title to a property is known as:

a. Suit of title

b. Chain of title

c. Blockchain

d. Deeds line

Answer B

Most registered properties in the USA have a chain of title-this is essentially a chronological list of all the transfers of the property or title. It helps identify the previous homeowners of the property.

59. The Desktop Underwriter is an automated underwriting system for which agency?

a. Freddie Mac

b. Fannie Mae

c. HUD

d. National Housing Association

Answer B

DU is an automated tool that can provide lenders with certainty early on through a comprehensive risk assessment, which determines a loan's eligibility for sale and delivery to Fannie Mae. DU is the powerhouse that connects Fannie Mae technologies and gives users innovation at their fingertips. 1.6 million

60. What is the major difference between Fannie Mae and Freddie mac?

a. Fannie Mae is a larger corporation compared to Freddie Mac

b. Fannie Mae buys mortgages from larger banks

c. Freddie Mae is only for first-time buyers

d. Only Freddie Mae offers insured loans

Answer B

The one major difference between Fanie Mae and Freddie Mac is where these agencies obtain their mortgages- meaning the source. In general, it appears that Fannie Mae purchases loans from larger financial institutions, whereas Freddie Mac purchases the mortgages from small banks.

61. What does a 96 loan to value mean?

a. The Borrower needs to put 96% down payment

b. The borrower needs to put in a 4% down payment

c. The borrower needs to put down 20% to get a loan of 96%

d. The borrower can only get a 4% loan

Answer B

Conventional 97 home loan lets you borrow 97% of the home's value, so you'll only have to put 3% down. If your credit is pretty good and you want an affordable low down payment alternative to an FHA mortgage, a Conventional 97 home loan might be worth considering.

62. Which of the following is not a good loan-to-value ratio?

a. 10%

b. 36%

c. 41%

d. 90%

Answer D

In general, the LTV should be low. The higher the LTV, the lower the risk of getting a loan. An LTV of 80% or higher is deemed too high for lenders to offer loans.

63. What does an automated underwriting system do?

a. Checks client's financial information

b. Does a background check for crime

c. It tabulates the amount of the down payment

d. It ensures that there is no discrimination in loans

Answer A

Automated underwriting systems (AUS) analyze a client's financial information (such as credit score and income) in addition to the overall value of the property they are looking to purchase

64. On page 2 of the loan estimate, what information will you usually find?

a. Services you should not shop for

b. Costs at closing

c. Loan terms

d. Estimated monthly principal and interest

Answer A

The loan estimate is a 3 page document; the second page reveals all the costs associated with processing, originating and underwriting. The second page also lists a list of services that borrowers 'can shop for' and 'cannot shop for.'

65. What is the penalty for an individual who violates the Gramm Leach Bliley Act?

a. $100K fine

b. $10,000 fine

c. Ten years incarceration

d. $100K fine and ten years in prison

Answer B

If an individual violates the Gramm Bliley act, he or she could face a monetary penalty of $10,000. Larger institutions and banks can face monetary penalties of $100,000 for each violation. Plus, individuals who violate the GLB Act can even be incarcerated for up to 5 years.

66. What is a temporary 2-1 buydown?

a. A concession offered by the seller to make low payments for the first two years

b. A concession made by the lender where there is no interest on the loan for the first two years

c. A concession made by the buyer who doubles the monthly payment for the first two years

d. A concession made by the bank where the buyer makes no payment for the first two years

Answer A

A 2-1 buydown program is a concession offered by sellers to incentivize buyers. A 2-1 buydown essentially allows borrowers to make a lower mortgage payment for the first two years of their loan, and payments go back up on the third year of the loan.

67. A legal process that is sometimes used to clarify or confirm property ownership is known as?

a. Suit of quiet title

b. Lien disclosure

c. Deed conflict

d. Title Resolution

Answer A

A suit of quiet title is a legal process that can help determine the property ownership. For example if there are any challenges to the title, a suit of quiet title can quickly resolve the issues of ownership.

68. How many pages are there in the closing disclosure?

a. 2

b. 3

c. 4

d. 5

Answer D

The closing disclosure is a five-page document that explains the final terms of the mortgage loan — and where all of your money will go. Prior to closing, the numbers you've been getting about your interest rate, monthly mortgage payments, property taxes, and more have been mere estimates.

69. How many pages is the Loan estimate?

a. 2

b. 3

c. 4

d. 5

Answer B

A Loan Estimate is a relatively small document consisting of 3 pages. It is given to the applicant after applying for a loan. The Loan Estimate contains important information about the loan that the borrower has applied for.

70. How long is a loan estimate valid for?

a. Three days

b. Five days

c. Ten days

d. 2 weeks

Answer C

All Loan estimates have an expiration date; this date is usually on the first page, near the heading. Loan Estimates are generally valid for ten business days from the date of issue.

71. In general, a loan estimate is only required for?

a. Residential homes

b. Reverse mortgages

c. Home equity line of credit

d. Manufactured housing loans that are not secured

Answer A

Loan estimates usually are not needed for reverse mortgages, home equity lines of credit (HELOCs), and manufactured housing loans that have not been not secured by the property.

72. What is a 203 b loan?

a. A loan for low-income families to purchase homes

b. A loan given to veterans who are chronically disabled

c. A loan given for purchase and home repair at the same time

d. Another name for a balloon loan

Answer C

An FHA 203(k) loan is used to assist home buyers who are purchasing a home in need of significant repairs or modifications.

73. What is a 203 k loan?

a. A rehabilitation loan

b. A loan to purchase a small business

c. A loan to purchase a secondary home

d. A loan for an agricultural business

Answer A

An FHA 203(k) loan is a government-backed mortgage that is essentially a construction loan that finances both the purchase and repairs of a home.

74. How many months of PITI payments must be verified for a loan on a non-owner-occupied property?

a. Two months

b. Four months

c. Six months

d. Nine months

Answer C

For a non-owner-occupied property, the lender will usually ask for PITI payments for up to 6 months. The PITI reserves must equal the sum that the homeowner borrowed to pay for the interest, principal, insurance and taxes for a defined time period after closing. For example, the lender may ask for 4 months of PITI reserves; if PITI equals $3,000 a month, the borrower must prove that he or she has liquid assets of $3,000 x 4= $12,000.

75. How many months of PITI payments must be verified for a loan on an owner-occupied property?

a. Two months

b. Four months

c. Six months

d. Nine months

Answer A

For an owner occupied property, usually two months of PITI payments are verified, but lenders are at liberty to ask for up to six months.

76. What percent of ownership do you need to have to be self-employed??

a. 10%

b. 25%

c. 50%

d. 70%

Answer B

If a person has 25% or more interest or ownership in an entity (e.g. business), then he or she can be considered to be self-employed.

77. How many years of review of the credit and public record information does Fannie Mae require?

a. Two years

b. Five years

c. Seven years

d. Ten years

Answer C

In general, when applying for a loan, Fannie Mae does require all the public and credit record information over a 7 year period. If the individual has filed for a bankruptcy in the past, the review looks at 10 years of records.

78. What is the minimum downpayment for an FHA loan if the borrower's credit score is 580?

a. 3.5%

b. 7%

c. 10%

d. 20%

Answer A

For an FHA loan the criteria for a loan are mild. The minimum downpayment for a FHA loan is only 3.5% of the total value of the property. Even the costs of the loan are much less than a conventional loan.

79. At what credit score is a borrower not eligible for an FHA loan?

a. Below 500

b. Below 550

c. Below 580

d. Below 600

Answer A

Even though FHA loans are relatively easy to come by, the minimum credit score must not be lower than 500. Individuals with scores higher than 500 are eligible for loans with minimal down payment.

80. What is the late fee for a VA loan?

a. 1%

b. 2%

c. 3%

d. 4%

Answer D

The late fee on a VA loan is 4% of the total fee. In addition, if the payment on the late fee is later than 30%, the VA will add on interest to the penalty. Very rarely is this penalty waived unless the borrower has extenuating circumstances.

81. What is the late fee for an FHA loan?

a. 1%

b. 2%

c. 3%

d. 4%

Answer D

For borrowers who are late with their monthly payments on a FHA loan, the late fee is 4%. Very rarely is this penalty waived unless the borrower has extenuating circumstances.

82. What is the front-end ratio for FHA loans?

a. 26%

b. 31%

c. 36%

d. 41%

Answer B

To be eligible for a FHA loan, the borrower must have a front-end ratio of 31%. In addition, a higher emphasis is placed on the back-end ratio, which should not be more than 43%. Some exceptions do exist depending on the individual's credit history.

83. What is the back-end ratio for FHA loans?

a. 26%

b. 30%

c. 36%

d. 43%

Answer D

To be eligible for a FHA loan, the borrower must have a front-end ratio of 31%. In addition, a higher emphasis is placed on the back-end ratio, which should not be more than 43%. Some exceptions do exist depending on the individual's credit history.

84. An applicant can request a statement of reasons within how many days of receiving the original adverse notice?

a. 14 days

b. 25 days

c. 45 days

d. 60 days

Answer D

After a borrower receives an adverse action letter, he or she has 60 days to request a FREE copy of the report from the credit agency. The name and address of the credit agency that was used are always stated in the denial letter.

85. If an applicant for credit is denied based on the appraisal, the borrower has how many days to request a copy of the letter?

a. 14 days

b. 25 days

c. 45 days

d. 90 days

Answer D

If the borrower is denied a loan based on an appraisal, he or she has 90 days to request a copy of the denial letter.

86. If an applicant for credit is denied based on the appraisal, the lender has to deliver the letter within what time period after the request has been made by the borrower?

a. Seven days

b. Fourteen days

c. Twenty-one days

d. Thirty days

Answer D

After obtaining all the relevant information on the borrower's credit and denying the loan, the creditor has 30 days in which to notify the borrower of the decision.

87. The primary function of ECOA is to?

a. Manage credit applications

b. Prohibit discrimination

c. Ensure lenders disclose information

d. Ensure borrowers get the cheapest loans

Answer B

The Equal Credit Opportunity Act (ECOA) was introduced primarily to ban all types of discrimination by lenders when offering loans. The ECOA applies to all types of financial transactions including extension of credit to corporations, small businesses, trusts and partnerships.

88. What is the meaning of 'servicing transfer?

a. Borrower gets the loan from another lender

b. Borrower sends payment to a different company

c. Lender refers a borrower to another servicer

d. Lender charges fees for services

Answer B

As a borrower, all a servicing transfer means is that you'll send your payments to a different company. That company will now also handle your escrow account, answer questions about your loan, and manage the foreclosure process if you default on the payments.

89. What is the late fee for a USDA loan?

a. 1%

b. 2%

c. 3%

d. 4%

Answer D

A late fee is assessed if full payment is not received within 15 days of the payment due date. The late fee is calculated at 4 percent of the customer's portion of the principal and interest payment due on the account unless state law requires a different rate.

90. What is the late fee for a conventional loan?

a. 1%

b. 2%

c. 5%

d. 6%

Answer C

The majority of lenders have a late fee of about 5% on late payments made on a conventional loan.

91. What is the front-end ratio for conventional loans?

a. 28%

b. 32%

c. 36%

d. 41%

Answer A

For conventional loans, lenders may look at both the front-end and back-end ratios to determine eligibility. The front end ratio for a conventional loan should be more than 28%. At the same time, the back end ratio should not be more than 36%.

92. What is the back-end ratio for conventional loans?

a. 28%

b. 36%

c. 41%

d. 44%

Answer B

In general, to be eligible for a conventional loan, the back end ratio must be 36% or lower. In rare cases individuals with back end ratios close to 50% may also be eligible provided they have a steady job and an excellent credit score.

93. What is the front-end ratio for USDA loans?

a. 29%

b. 36%

c. 40%

d. 44%

Answer A

To be eligible for a USDA loan, the borrower must have a front end ratio of 29%. The housing ratio looks at the ratio of the monthly mortgage payments and compares it with the gross monthly income.

94. What is the back-end ratio for a USDA loan?

a. 29%

b. 36%

c. 41%

d. 44%

Answer C

Lenders will calculate your back-end DTI ratio by looking at all of your major monthly expenses, including your new projected housing payment. The USDA guideline is 41 percent, although it's possible to exceed that and still obtain a USDA-backed loan.

95. What is the back-end ratio for a VA loan?

a. 26%

b. 36%

c. 41%

d. 44%

Answer C

VA loans allow for a maximum 41% back-end debt-to-income ratio. This means your total monthly debts, including your projected VA mortgage payment, can't exceed 41% of your monthly pre-tax income.

96. In general, in a high-priced mortgage, the interest will usually exceed the APOR by how many percentage points?

a. 1%

b. 2.5%

c. 5%

d. 10%

Answer B

It is a first-lien jumbo mortgage with an APR that exceeds the APOR published by the CFPB at the time the APR is set by 2.5 percentage points or more.

97. A section 35 loan only applies to?

a. Residential dwellings

b. Commercial building

c. Agriculture enterprise

d. Warehouses

Answer A

A Section 35 loan only applies to one to four unit owner occupied residential property. The dwelling can be a multi-unit or a single unit home, irrespective of whether the dwelling is attached to the property.

98. In general, a section 35 loan is also known as a:

a. Low-priced mortgage loan

b. Non-conforming loan

c. Predatory loan

d. High priced loan for personal property

Answer D

A Section 35 loan only applies to one to four unit owner occupied residential property. The dwelling can be a multi-unit or a single unit home, irrespective of whether the dwelling is attached to the property.

99. What is the key importance of the Gramm Leach Bliley Act?

a. Minimize discrimination when it comes to loans

b. Lenders need to reveal the exact cost of the loan

c. Encourage lenders to refer borrowers for low-priced loans

d. Lenders must explain to borrowers the information-sharing practices

Answer D

The Gramm-Leach-Bliley Act was introduced to make lenders and financial institutions more responsible and accountable. The act made it mandatory that no matter what type of financial service the company was offering, it had to explain to the borrower all its information sharing practices. The goal was to protect client personal information.

Practice Test 4

1. The ultimate decision maker on whether to grant the applicant a loan is the:

a. Servicer

b. Lender

c. Underwriter

d. Bank

Answer C

The underwriter is the ultimate individual who determines whether the applicant gets a mortgage. Underwriters usually assess the credit and financial history of the applicant to determine if they are a high-risk borrower.

2. Which governmental branch was responsible for implementing TILA?

a. Federal Reserve Board

b. Federal TC

c. FCRA

d. FHA

Answer A

In 1968, Congress passed The Truth in Lending Act (TILA). The primary aim of this law was to educate and protect consumers when dealing with creditors and lenders. The Federal Reserve Board played a key role in implementing TILA.

3. What is a section 35 loan?

a. Low-interest loan

b. High-priced loan

c. Fixed interest loan

d. Interest-free loan

Answer B

In general, a section 35 loan is a high-priced loan; this closed-end loan is secured by personal property or a one-to-four-unit owner-occupied residential property or personal property; the key feature is that it must be the principal residence of the borrower.

4. The Financial Service Modernization Act of 1999 is also known as?

a. RESPA

b. FACTA

c. FCRA

d. Gramm Leach Bliley Act

Answer D

The Financial Services Modernization Act is also known as the Gramm-Leach-Bliley Act. The Act was passed by Congress in 1999 to deregulate the financial industry.

5. When should the borrower receive the servicing transfer statement?

a. Not more than 15 days after the transfer date

b. Three days after the effective transfer date

c. 30 days after the effective transfer

d. At anytime

Answer A

The service transfer document should be provided to the borrower not more than 2 weeks (or 15 days) after the effective date of the transfer of the account.

6. In general, how many service transfer notices should be sent to the borrower?

a. 1

b. 2

c. 4

d. 5

Answer B

When the borrower has a new servicer, they should be provided with a minimum of two notices. The service transfer document should be sent to the borrower 15 days before the effective transfer date. In addition, a notice should be provided by the new servicer within two weeks after the effective transfer date.

7. After the service transfer document, how long can the borrower continue to make payments to the old servicer?

a. 15 days

b. 30 days

c. 45 days

d. 60 days

Answer D

Even after receiving the service transfer notice, the borrower can continue to make payments to the old service for 60 days- this is considered the grace period after a service transfer. The new servicer cannot treat the payments to the old servicer as late if made within 60 days.

8. A 203 G loan is also referred to as the:

a. Good neighbor next door loan

b. High-priced loan

c. Energy efficient loan

d. Condominium loan

Answer A

The 203G loan is part of the FHA loan program. Most importantly, the FHA loan program is geared towards encouraging community reinvestment. The 203G loan is also referred to as the Good neighbor next door loan.

9. Generally, a 203G loan is for which group of people?

a. Disabled individuals

b. Active veterans

c. Minorities

d. Firefighters and paramedics

Answer D

A 203G loan is part of the FHA program, which focuses on reinvesting in the community. This particular loan is strictly for paramedics, law enforcement, firefighters, teachers, etc. The 203 g loans are often known as the Officer and Teacher Next Door program. The homes are available at reduced prices with a very low down payment.

10. If a consumer requests cancellation of their escrow account, the lender must deliver an escrow closing notice no later than how many days before the closure of the account?

a. Within three business days

b. Within five business days

c. Within 15 business days

d. Within 30 business days

Answer A

As with most notices, the lenders usually have three business days to deliver the escrow Closing notice.

11. If the escrow account is canceled by someone other than the consumer, the lender must deliver the escrow closing notice within how many days before the account is closed?

a. Three business days

b. Five business days

c. 15 business days

d. 30 business days

Answer D

However, suppose the escrow account is closed by someone other than the borrower or not at the request of the consumer. In that case, the lender has 30 business days to send the notice.

12. On average, telemarketers should honor the 'do not call list' for how long?

a. Three months

b. Six months

c. 12 months

d. Five years

Answer D

Under federal law, telemarketers must honor the do not call list for five years. This number does vary in some states from 2 to 5 years.

13. What is functional obsolescence in real estate?

a. Diminished interest in the buyer's taste

b. Home with limited functionalities

c. An older home that cannot be renovated

d. Cheap home

Answer A

This is known as functional obsolescence, when the buyer loses interest in the property or the home is no longer appealing. The loss of interest may be because the property is old, outdated, and can no longer be upgraded.

14. A certificate of eligibility is required for an applicant who is applying for which type

of loan?

a. USDA

b. FHA

c. VA

d. Jumbo loan

Answer C

When veterans apply for a VA loan, they first need to show a certificate of eligibility. This means they need to show the lender that they actually served in the armed forces or the military. Without this certificate of eligibility, a VA loan cannot be issued.

15. Which federal Regulation encourages banks and lenders to meet the credit needs of their community, especially in low-income neighborhoods?

a. Community Reinvestment act

b. Home Mortgage Disclosure Act

c. HOEPA

d. TILA

Answer A

The 1977 Community Reinvestment Act was enacted for several reasons, but the key reason was to encourage banks and lenders to offer credit to the low and middle-income communities in the local communities where they operate. The aim of the CRA was to help low-income families purchase homes.

16. What is the meaning of the abbreviation 'DTI?'

a. Debt transaction inquiry

b. Debt to income ratio

c. Due time income

d. Differential Time Income

Answer B

The debt-to-income ratio is widely used by lenders to determine eligibility for a mortgage. In simple terms, one totals the total debt each month and divides it by the monthly income. Individuals with high DTIs usually are not eligible for loans as they carry too much debt. But other factors like credit score and downpayment also come into play before a decision is made on loan approval.

17. Prevention of predatory lending is the key focus of which federal agency?

a. HOEPA

b. CFPB

c. TILA

d. FCRA

Answer A

In the past, predatory and deceptive lending practices were common in the lending industry. However, several laws, including HOEPA, have been passed to prevent fraud in real estate. In 2008, many owners lost their homes and savings as a result of predatory lending practices.

18. Which is the only loan program that requires an upfront mortgage insurance premium?

a. VA Loan

b. USDA Loan

c. ARM Loan

d. FHA Loan

Answer D

In general, FHA loans only require a downpayment of 3.5% of the home's value. And while the eligibility for FHA loans is less stringent, the borrower must come up with upfront mortgage insurance, which in most cases is asked for at the time of Closing.

19. In general, how many VA loans can one have at any point in time?

a. One

b. Two

c. Three

d. No limit

Answer B

The general limit is two as long as one can prove that there are two distinct primary dwellings. However, the borrower must have good credit scores, a stable job, and a history of making timely monthly payments on past loans. Most people are turned down for the second mortgage until they prove they can make payments on both loans.

20. Ethics is a common subject in exams. What percentage of questions are based on this subject?

a. 2-4%

b. 5-7

c.12-16%

d. >25%

Answer C

In general, expect to see at least 5-10 questions on ethics in the exam. The percentage of ethics questions does vary on each test, but it is a major topic that is heavily tested.

21. The Real Estate Settlement Procedures Act is also referred to as Regulation?

a. X

b. C

c. D

d. M

Answer A

Regulation X is a provision of RESPA. It requires mortgage brokers, lenders, or services of mortgages to provide borrowers with timely and relevant disclosures about the loan. The disclosures should reveal the cost and nature of the home-buying process. Regulation X also bars deceptive practices like kickbacks and referrals for money.

22. Section 10 of RESPA pertains to which of the following?

a. Fraud

b. Deceptive practices

c. Escrow accounts

d. Identity thefts

Answer C

Section 10 of the Real Estate Settlement Procedures Act (RESPA) protects borrowers from lenders; specifically, section 10 ensures that lenders do not ask for unusually large sums of money in the escrow account for paying taxes and insurance.

23. Which of the following is not part of a trust?

a. A trustee

b. A Beneficiary

c. A Trustor

d. A Guarantor

Answer D

A Trust has five key entities: the grantor, trustee, beneficiary, assets, trustee, and terms. A guarantor is not part of the trust.

24. When the lender is able to seize the collateral but unable to seize the property, this is known as:

a. Non-recourse agreement

b. Conveyance

c. Reverse conveyance

d. Forfeiture

Answer A

With a Non Recourse Agreement, the lender is able to seize the collateral but will not be able to seize property. In many loan contracts, a non-recourse agreement may be stated in small writing.

25. After chapter 7, how long does the borrower have to wait before he or she is eligible for a mortgage?

a. Two years

b. Five years

c. Seven years

d. Ten years

Answer C

In general, after chapter 7, most lenders will delay loaning any money for at least two years. Some lenders may be willing to loan money early, but these loans come with very high-interest rates. Scams are common when it comes to refinancing after chapter 7 and chapter 11.

26. After a short sale, if you are willing to put down less than 20%, how long must the borrower wait to get a new mortgage?

a.12 months

b. 24 months

c. 36 months

d. 48 months

Answer D

If the property has been through a short sale, then the borrower usually will have to wait before he or she will be eligible for a loan. The amount of time the borrower may have to wait to get a mortgage depends on the down payment. If the down payment is 20% or less, the wait is at least four years, and with less than 10% down, the wait is at least seven years.

27. Under the Fair Credit and Reporting Act, consumers have the right to receive how many free credit reports each year?

a. 1

b. 2

c. 3

d. 5

Answer A

According to the FCRA, consumers can get one free credit report from one of the three credit agencies.

28. The Fair and Accurate Credit Transaction Act (FACTA) is an amendment to which federal Act?

a. FCRA

b. FACTA

c. TILA

d. RESPA

Answer A

FACTA is an amendment to the Fair Credit Reporting Act.

29. The primary goal of The Fair and Accurate Credit Transaction Act is to:

a. Ensure accuracy of consumer credit reports

b. Ensure that credit agencies do not push too many credit cards

c. That there is no discrimination in eligibility for credit cards

d. Allows consumers to get multiple free copies of their credit report each year

Answer A

The Fair and Accurate Credit Transactions Act (FACTA) was passed in 2003, specifically in response to the epidemic of identity thefts in the financial and credit industry. In addition, FACTA also protected consumers by insisting that credit agencies provide accurate credit reports.

30. Under FACTA, the 'safeguard' rule requires that all documents must be stored for what period of time before they are destroyed?

a. One year

b. Two years

c. Three years

d. Five years

Answer B

Under FACTA, the safeguard rule requires that all lenders and creditors maintain and store customer financial and personal information safely for a minimum of 24 months after the last the information was used.

31. The 'Disposal Rule' is part of which Federal Act:

a. FACTA

b. FCRA

c. FTC

d. FDA

Answer A

FACTA has introduced the Disposal Rule to ensure that customer documents are safely and securely stored. The goal of the disposal rule is to make sure that the accounts are not easily hacked. It should not be possible for anyone to access consumer credit and personal data.

32. Which of the following is not a type of appraisal in real estate?

a. Cost approach

b. Sales comparison

c. Income approach

d. Location approach

Answer D

There are many ways to appraise real estate properties, but the three key methods include the cost approach, income approach, and sales approach. The location approach is not an appraisal method.

33. When using a sales comparison to appraise a property, the comparable property must be within what distance of the subject property?

a. 100 feet

b. Half a mile

c. One mile

d. Within sight of vision

Answer C

In general, when comparing property values or doing appraisals, the comparable property must be located within 1 mile of the subjective home.

34. The legal right to utilize another person's land for a limited time or a specific purpose is known as?

a. Easement

b. Encasement

c. Infringement

d. Entrapment

Answer A

Sometimes one property owner may grant permission to an adjacent property owner to use his land. For example, sometimes, one owner may share his driveway; this type of Easement or sharing is common in rural areas. By allowing the other owner to use the land, the dominant owner can be assured that there will be no other major infringements on the property (e.g., building a new driveway).

35. When a restrictive covenant is a clause in a leased property, it usually means?

a. The owner can rent out the rooms

b. The owner is at liberty to do any type of renovation

c. The owner may only make small modifications in the home

d. The owner has to share the rental profits with the landlord

Answer C

In most rentals and leased properties, there is a restrictive covenant- meaning that the tenant cannot make any major changes to the building or property.

36. When a property owner violates the property rights of the adjacent neighbor by building or allowing something to hang over the neighbor's property, this is known as:

a. Easement

b. Infiltration

c. Encroachment

d. Interfering

Answer C

Encroachment is a common problem in real estate. This occurs when one owner violates the neighbor's property by building a fence or extending his garden over the property lines of the neighbor.

37. When two people have co-ownership of a property with an undivided interest but have no right to survivorship, this is known as:

a. Tenancy in common

b. Joint Tenancy

c. Right to survivorship

d. Tenancy by the entirety

Answer A

With Tenancy in common, the two people have co-ownership of the property with undivided interest. But if one of the owners dies, the property does not automatically pass over to the other partner; instead, it becomes part of the estate.

38. When there is co-ownership by a couple who are legally married, and each has an equal and undivided share of the property, this is known as:

a. Tenancy in common

b. Joint Tenancy

c. Right to survivorship

d. Tenancy by entirety

Answer D

Tenancy by entirety is where there is co-ownership by a couple who are married, and each partner has an equal and even share of the home. However, in order to modify the home, consent from both partners is necessary. If one partner dies, the property then belongs to the living spouse.

39. The maximum flood insurance one can obtain from the Federal National Flood Insurance Program (NFIP) for the property is:

a. 100K

b. 150K

c. 200K

d. 250K

Answer D

In general, there is a limit on how much flood insurance one can get from NFIP. For residential homes, the maximum coverage is $250K and $100K for personal property. Of course, one can buy more insurance but only from private agencies.

40. If the borrower has a total monthly income of $6,000 and housing expenses of $2500, his front-end ratio will be?

a. 28%

b. 31%

c. 36%

d. 41.6%

Answer D

To calculate the front-end ratio, divide the total housing expenses by the total monthly income; thus, 2,500/6,000= 41.6%

41. What is the term for the legal provision that allows one to eliminate legal liability in certain scenarios, provided certain conditions are met?

a. Honest Deception

b. Safe Harbor

c. Scott Free

d. Passive stealing

Answer B

The term Safe Harbor is a legal provision that helps people eliminate or avoid regulatory or legal liability in specific scenarios; the key is that one has to meet these conditions first.

42. Violations of the Home Ownership and Equity Protection Act (HOEPA) are presently enforced by which of the following federal agencies:

a. FTC

b. CFPB

c. RESPA

d. FBI.

Answer B

The majority of violations in the financial and real estate industry are enforced by CFPB (Consumer Financial Protection Bureau).

43. The Home Ownership and Equity Protection Act covers which of the following loans:

a. Reverse mortgages.

b. Loans on second homes

c. Home equity loans

d. A new construction loan.

Answer C

The 1994 Home Ownership and Equity Protection Act (HOEPA) is an amendment to the Truth in Lending Act (TILA); the key goal of HOEPA is to protect consumers from deceptive and fraudulent practices in the mortgage industry. HOEPA covers home equity loans and other high-priced loans; it does not cover construction loans, loans for vacation or second homes, or reverse mortgages.

44. Which statement best defines a balloon payment?

a. Involves one large payment at the beginning

b. Involves a final lump sum of 50% of the loan

c. Involves a payment that is much bigger at the end compared to the beginning

d. Involves a lump sum that is the same as the initial payment

Answer C

A balloon payment is essentially a lump sum principal balance that is paid at the end of a loan term. The payments are very low in the beginning, but a large sum is required to pay off the loan at the end.

45. Private mortgage insurance is primarily dealt under which federal law?

a. TILA

b. RESPA

c. HPA

d. FTC

Answer C

The 1998 Homeowners Protection Act was passed by Congress to help decrease unnecessary insurance payments by homeowners. In the past, lenders continued to demand insurance payments even though the insurance was no longer needed.

46. As per the Homeowners Protection Act (HPA), the private mortgage insurance on the borrower's loan can be automatically canceled at what point in time?

a. When the loan is 80% or less of the original value.

b. When the borrower asks

c. When the borrower has home equity of 10%.

d. When the borrower is consistent with his payments for 24 months

Answer A

According to the HPA, once the borrower's home equity reaches 20% or the loan-to-value ratio is 80%. At this point, the insurance should be automatically canceled. Previously, homeowners could not get the lender to cancel the insurance.

47. Which one of the following loans reflects a section 35 loan?

a. High Priced Loan

b. Jumbo loan

c. Reverse mortgage

d. VA loan

Answer A

In general, a section 35 loan is a high-priced loan; it is essentially a closed-end loan that is frequently secured by the consumer's primary dwelling. In addition, the APR on this loan often is greater than the average prime rate.

48. The primary goal of the Equal Credit Opportunity Act is:

a. Ensure lenders disclose all the loan information

b. Ensure that there is no identity theft

c. Ensure lenders do not charge exorbitant interest on loans

d. Ensure that there is no discrimination in the lending industry

Answer D

The key aim of the Equal Credit Opportunity Act (ECOA) is to bar discrimination in all financial and credit transactions; the ECOA applies to all types of credit associated with corporations, businesses, trusts and partnerships.

49. In general, according to the Equal Credit Opportunity Act, a borrower must be notified of the lending decision by a creditor within what time period after completing the application?

a. Three days

b. Seven days

c. 15 days

d. 30 days

Answer D

After completing a loan application, the creditor has the onus of notifying the applicant about the results-whether adverse or favorable, within 30 days after the application was completed.

50. Prior to receiving the mortgage contract, what is the name of the document that the borrower receives from the lender signifying that financing has been approved?

a. Letter of commitment

b. Loan document

c. Letter of acknowledgment

d. Good faith document

Answer A

Before a borrower receives the total mortgage contract, he or she will receive a letter of commitment- also referred to as an approval letter. The Letter of Commitment reveals that the borrower has been approved for financing and will go into effect after the contract is signed. The Letter of Commitment will also outline the conditions and terms of the loan.

51. When an application is denied a loan, according to ECOA, the lender should issue what Letter?

a. Fail notice

b. A statement of mortgage decline

c. An adverse action statement

d. A letter of apology

Answer C

When a loan is declined, the creditor or servicer will often send the applicant an adverse action statement. At the same time, the names and addresses of the credit agencies that supplied the credit report will be stated.

52. Borrowers, according to ECOA, can request a copy of the appraisal report used to make the loan decision in what time period?

a. 15 days

b. 30 days

c. 90 days

d. 120 days

Answer C

A borrower can make a request for the appraisal report in writing once a decision has been made on the loan, but this must be done within 90 days.

53. The primary aim of the Home Mortgage Disclosure Act is to:

a. Ensure all loan disclosures are made to the borrower

b. Ensure that there is an escrow account

c. Prevent discrimination in the lending industry

d. Keep all the relevant financial records

Answer D

In 1975, the Home Mortgage Disclosure Act (HMDA) was passed by Congress in order to bring more accountability and transparency to the residential mortgage industry. Creditors and lenders are now mandated to maintain certain financial documents for several years.

54. Violations of the Home Mortgage Disclosure Act are enforced by which federal agency?

a. FTC

b. HUD

c. CFPB

d. FACTA

Answer C

In general, most financial and credit violations are enforced by the Consumer Financial Protection Bureau.

55. Regulation C is also known as:

a. RESPA

b. TILA

c. HMDA

d. ECOA

Answer C

Regulation C is the same as the Home Mortgage Disclosure Act. The Regulation mandates that financial institutions report, collect, and disclose specific information about their mortgage lending activity.

56. Home Mortgage Disclosure Act applies to which of the following covered properties?

a. Vacant land

b. New construction

c. Home purchase

d. Loans for pools

Answer C

The HMDA, in general, applies to one-to-four-family residential properties. However, it does not apply to new instructions, vacant land, or loans sold as part of a servicing pool.

57. Regulation V is also known as:

a. Fair Credit Reporting Act

b. Home Mortgage Disclosure Act

c. The Fair and Accurate Credit Transactions Act

d. Gramm Leach Bliley Act

Answer A

The Fair Credit Reporting Act is designed to protect consumer rights. It has imposed many rules and responsibilities on lending institutions and credit agencies, including providing accurate credit reports. It is also known as Regulation V.

58. What is it called when a builder who has many unsold units in a condominium complex uses fraudulent schemes to sell the properties?

a. Dumping

b. Builder bailout

c. Ponzi scheme

d. Selling lemons

Answer B

Builder bailout is a common scheme when properties do not sell. This fraudulent scheme is often used by builders who utilize various fraudulent methods to sell remaining units.

59. What is it called when a mortgage servicer continues to foreclose a homeowner's property while at the same time considering loan modification of the homeowner's application?

a. Builder bailout

b. Occult foreclosure

c. Dual tracking

d. False hopes

Answer C

Sometimes a mortgage servicer will continue to foreclose on the homeowner's property but at the same time will be considering the homeowner's application for modification in the loan- this is known as dual tracking. Dual tracking can lead to a delay in the foreclosure process.

60. When is the initial escrow account statement due from the servicer?

a. Within three business days

b. Within seven days

c. Within 30 days

d. Within 45 days

Answer D

In general, the servicer has to submit an initial escrow account statement to the borrower within 45 business days after the date the escrow account was opened.

61. What is it called when an owner's policy or loan policy is insuring the same real estate property and contains the same effective date?

a. Forgery

b. Simultaneous Issue

c. Clerical error

d. Deception

Answer B

Simultaneous Issue means an owner's leasehold policy, owner's home policy, or loan policy are all insuring the same real estate property and at the same effective calendar dates.

62. What does GNMA stand for?

a. Government National Mortgage Association

b. Government of New Mexico Association

c. Guaranteed National Mortgage Act

d. Growing National Mortgage Association

Answer A

The Government National Mortgage Association, also known as Ginnie Mae, is a government branch within HUD (Department of Housing and Urban Development). It was created in 1968 when Fannie Mae was privatized. The mission of Ginnie Mae is to broaden funding for loans that are guaranteed or insured by the federal government.

63. What is one key difference between Fannie Mae and Ginnie Mae?

a. Fannie Mae is owned by the government

b. Ginnie Mae is owned by the government

c. Ginnie Mae does not issue loans

d. Fannie Mae only insures loans

Answer B

One major difference between Fannie Mae and Ginnie Mae is that the latter is owned by the US Government. Ginnie Mae is part of HUD, whereas both Freddie Mac and Fannie Mae are private agencies.

64. Which loan is not guaranteed by Ginnie Mae?

a. VA

b. USDA

c. FHA

d. HOEPA

Answer D

Ginnie Mae guarantees USDA loans, VA loans, FHA loans, and the Section 184 loan program to help Native Americans acquire homeownership.

65. What does the abbreviation AUS stand for in real estate?

a. Automatic Update Server

b. Automatic User service

c. Automated Underwriting System

d. Automated Unified Server

Answer C

Many mortgage lenders use an automated underwriting service to determine whether to approve a loan. These automated underwriting programs are fast and provide a decision in a matter of minutes.

66. If the landlord delivers a letter to the tenant that he or she is selling the property where the tenant is residing, this document is known as?

a. Letter to move

b. Eviction notice

c. Estoppel letter

d. Termination of contract

Answer C

The estoppel certificate, in the context of real estate, is usually delivered by the landlord to the tenant when the former is either selling or financing the property where the tenant resides.

67. What is the name of the document that transfers the property title from the owner to the lender in exchange for mortgage debt relief?

a. Estoppel letter

b. Deed in lieu of foreclosure

C. Lien on property

d. Eviction note

Answer B

Sometimes the property title is transferred from the homeowner to the lender in exchange for relief from the mortgage payment. This document is known as the Deed in lieu of foreclosure.

68. The Loan Application Register is part of which Act or Regulation?

a. ECOA

b. RESPA

c. FHA

d. HMDA

Answer D

The LAR Formatting Tool was created to assist creditors and financial institutions in managing electronic files that can then be uploaded on the HMDA platform.

Practice Test 5

1. The Home Ownership and Equity Protection Act (HOEPA) was passed in 1994 as an amendment to which Federal Act?

a. RESPA

b. TILA

c. FHA

d. FACTA

Answer B

In 1994, Congress passed HOEPA as an amendment to the existing Truth in Lending Act (TILA)

2. HOEPA loans are also known as?

a. Second mortgages

b. Reverse mortgages

c. Jumbo loans

d. Section 32 loans

Answer D

For much of the past, HOEPA loans have been referred to as section 32 loans. In simple terms, these are high-cost mortgages.

3. The key reason why the Home Ownership and Equity Protection Act was passed was to:

a. Ensure that lenders provide credit to the local community

b. No discrimination

c. Ensure low-priced loans

d. Deter abusive practices in the lending industry

Answer D

HOEPA was enacted primarily to overcome the deceptive and abusive practices in closed-end home equity loans and refinances. These loans always came with exorbitant interest rates and/or high administrative and closing fees.

4. When lenders have an affiliated business arrangement, they are supposed to disclose this fact to the consumer when they own, at minimum, what percent of the referral entity?

a. 1%

b. 2%

c. 5%

d. 10%

Answer A

When a broker, real estate agent, or lender has, at minimum, an Affiliated business arrangement of 1%, he or she is supposed to disclose this fact to the consumer. The disclosure should be made prior to signing any documents.

5. According to the Civil Rights Act of 1964, lenders and financial institutions cannot discriminate against which group or class?

a. Age

b. Gender

c. Religion

d. Race

Answer D

The key aim of the civil rights act of 1964 was to prevent discrimination against African Americans. The Act underwent 11 additional amendments over the years and is now comprehensive and includes discrimination against age, religion, gender, etc.

6. What federal law deals with the advertising of loans to consumers?

a. Regulation Z/TILA

b. ECOA

c. Federal Housing Act

d. FACTA

Answer A

Any form of advertising, even if it is social media where creditors advertise financial or credit products, must comply with Regulation Z provisions.

7. A lender is prohibited from providing kickbacks because of which federal law?

a. RESPA

b. ECOA

c. HUD

d. FACTA

Answer A

The Real Estate Settlement Procedures Act (RESPA) of 1974 offers consumers clear disclosures of settlement costs and to lower the closing costs by getting rid of kickbacks and referral fees.

8. When the borrower's mortgage reaches an 80% loan-to-value ratio, which federal Regulation requires the lender to cancel the private mortgage insurance?

a. FCRA

b. Homeowners Protection Act

c. FACTA

d. FHA

Answer B

The Homeowners Protection Act mandates that private medical insurance must be automatically canceled when the homeowners have accumulated the necessary equity of 20% in their homes.

9. Under ECOA rules, if the borrower has the loan application approved, the appraisal report should be provided to the borrower within?

a. 3 days

b. 5 days

c. 7 days

d. 10 days

Answer A

In 2013, ECOA amended Regulation B -which mandated that creditors provide loan applicants and homebuyers with a free copy of the appraisal. This report must be received by the applicants within three business days.

10. Which agency governs the majority of conforming loans?

a. VA

b. USDA

c. FHA

d. Fannie Mae and Freddie Mac

Answer D

Conforming loans are ones that follow a set of rules established by the Federal Housing Finance agency. The majority of mortgages are conforming -meaning they are qualified to be bought and guaranteed by Freddie Mac and Fannie Mae.

11. A negative report can remain on the credit report for what period of time?

a. 2 years

b. 5 years

c. 7 years

d. 12 years

Answer C

In general, most negative data on the credit report remains for seven years.

12. How long can a bankruptcy remain on the credit report for that period of time?

a. 2 years

b. 5 years

c. 7 years

d. 10 years

Answer D

Once a bankruptcy has been filed, it will remain on the credit report for ten years.

13. When the PITI plus the monthly debt is divided by the gross monthly income, this is known as?

a. Front-end ratio

b. Back-end ratio

c. Total debt

d. Monthly premium

Answer B

The back-end ratio is easy to calculate; all one does is add all the borrower's monthly debt payments and divide the sum by the borrower's monthly income.

14. Creditors who comply with Regulation Z must retain the documents for what period of time?

a. 3 months

b. 6 months

c. 12 months

d. 2 years

Answer D

Outside of advertising, creditors who comply with Regulation Z must retain the relevant documents for at least two years.

15. When the PITI is divided by the gross monthly income, this is known as?

a. Housing ratio

b. Back-end ratio

c. Monthly premiums

d. Total debt

Answer A

The front-end ratio, also known as the housing ratio, is a percentage that is obtained by dividing the housing expenses by the monthly income. The ratio can reveal how much the borrower is paying for the home, and this number tells the lender if the borrower qualifies for a mortgage.

16. The annual percentage rate is also known as:

a. Effective rate

b. Note rate

c. Nominal rate

d. yearly rate

Answer A

The effective annual interest rate is the actual return on any interest-paying investment. It also reflects the real percentage rate owned on a loan or a credit card. It is also referred to as the effective rate.

17. What do the abbreviations MDIA stand for?

a. Mortgage Disclosure Improvement Act

b. Money Debt Investment Act

c. Mortgage Deficit Investment Act

d. Money Disclosure Interchange Act

Answer A

The Mortgage Disclosure Improvement Act was broadened in 2008 and added more disclosures for many more types of financial transactions. In addition, the Act also increased the waiting time between the consummation of transactions and disclosures.

18. Under which federal Regulation does the Mortgage Disclosure Improvement Act fall?

a. TILA,/Reg Z

b. RESPA

c. FACTA

d. FCRA

Answer A

The amendments to Regulation Z's disclosure requirements implement revisions to TILA made by MDIA.

19. Blockbusting falls under which federal Regulation?

a. Fair Housing Act

b. RESPA

c. ECOA

d. FACTA

Answer A

Under the Fair Housing Act, Blockbusting, also known as panic selling, is an illegal, discriminatory practice where real estate agents try to alter the racial pool of a neighborhood by encouraging sales and listings in that area.

20. Loans under section 32 fall under which federal Regulation?

a. FHA

b. TILA/Reg Z

c. RESPA

d. FACTA

Answer B

The rules for high-priced loans can be found in section 32 of Regulation Z, which implements TILA. These loans are also called section 32 loans because of their location in section 32.

21. Loans under section 35 fall under which federal Regulation?

a. FHA

b. TILA/Reg Z

c. RESPA

d. FACTA

Answer B

Section 35 loans are defined as closed-end loans that are secured by a one to four-unit owner-occupied residential property. These high-priced loans are under Regulation Z of TILa.

22. In general, high-priced loans fall under which federal Regulation?

a. FHA

b. TILA/Reg Z

c. RESPA

d. FACTA

Answer B

The majority of high-priced loans fall under TILA/Regulation Z.

23. HOEPA loans fall under which federal Regulation?

a. FHA

b. TILA/Reg Z

c. RESPA

d. FACTA

Answer B

HOEPA loans also fall under TILA/Regulation Z.

24. What is the definition of a high-priced loan?

a. A first-line mortgage with an APR that is 1.5 percentage points or more than the APOR

b. A first-line mortgage with an APOR that is 1.5 percentage points more than the APR

c. A first-line mortgage with an APR that is at least five percentage points higher than a conventional mortgage

d. A first-line mortgage with very high monthly interest rates that exceed the APOR by fourfold.

Answer A

In general, a first-line mortgage is "higher-priced" if the APR is 1.5 percentage points or more than the APOR.

25. Once a borrower has paid off all the debts and liens, the remaining value of the property is known as?

a. Benefits

b. Deed

c. Equity

d. Bonus

Answer C

Home equity is the differential between the home value and how much you own on the mortgage. For example, if your home is worth $500,000 and you owe $300,000 on the mortgage, your home equity is $200,000.

26. If the consumer wants to buy a home in a rural area, which governmental branch will loan out the money for such an endeavor?

a. VA

b. FHA

c. USDA

d. TILA

Answer C

For people wishing to buy a home in rural or suburban areas, they can apply for a USDA loan. These loans have zero down payments and are guaranteed by the USDA. Even borrowers with low income are eligible.

27. Which government branch is known to insure mortgages offered by lenders and banks?

a. FHA

b. VA

c. FCRA

d. FACTA

Answer A

FHA loans are regulated and insured by the Federal Housing Administration. The loan does not come directly from the FHA but from private lenders. The FHA simply insures it, which makes lenders eager to give them to consumers.

28. What is the terminology to describe the time period between the disbursal of your loan and the last equated monthly installment payment you made?

a. Loan paid off

b. Free title

c. Loan tenure

d. Balloon payment

Answer C

The tenure in a loan is the time period between the disbursal of your loan and the last EMI payment that you make. For example, if you took out a car loan that was disbursed on 1st February 2018 and you repaid the debt in its entirety on 1st February 2021, the loan tenure is three years.

29. If a borrower uses someone else's name to buy real estate, but that individual will not be residing at the property, this type of fraud scheme is known as?

a. Straw buyer

b. Redlining

c. Theft by deception

d. Identity theft

Answer A

A straw buyer is a person who purchases real estate on behalf of another person. Real estate agents may sometimes use a straw buyer when the real home buyer is unable to complete the financial transaction/ It is an illegal endeavor.

30. If the borrower has made an address change, the creditor must verify the validity of the change according to which Regulation?

a. Section 114 of the FACT Act

b. Regulation Z

c. Regulation C

d. FCRA

Answer A

The fair and accurate Credit Transaction act of 2003 was amended to prevent, detect and mitigate identity thefts. All address changes by the applicant must be verified.

31. Identity theft prevention is governed by which Federal Agency?

a. FCRA

b. Federal Trade Commission

c. FBI

d. TILA

Answer B

The Fair and Accurate Credit Transactions Act (FACTA) mandates that lenders and banks create and implement a written identity theft prevention program. The overall program is overseen by the FTC

32. Section 114 rules are a part of which Regulation?

a. FACT Act

b. FCRA

c. FBI

d. TILA

Answer A

Section 114 rules fall under FACT act, which was introduced to lower identity theft in the USA.

33. Lenders are prohibited from splitting fees associated with loans due to which federal Regulation?

a. RESPA

b. Gramm Bliley Act

c. TILA

d. Dodd-Frank Act

Answer A

The splitting of fees or kickbacks during real estate transactions is forbidden under RESPA. Unless there is an actual service performed, no money should be exchanged.

34. The Dodd-Frank Act and Consumer Finance Protection Act led to the creation of which federal agency?

a. CFPB

b. RESPA

c. TILA

d. FTC

Answer A

After the major housing crisis in 2008, the CFPB was created. It was the result of a combination of the Dodd-Frank Act and the Consumer Finance Protection Act.

35. Which Federal Act was created to ensure that federally insured banks and lenders

meet the credit needs of the local community with safe and secure banking practices?

a. Community Reinvestment Act

b. Fair Housing Act

c. Home Mortgage Disclosure Act

d. Equal Credit Opportunity Act

Answer A

The Community Reinvestment Act of 1977 was created to ensure that federally insured leaders and banks meet the credit needs of the local communities with safe and unbiased lending practices.

36. Which Act was passed in 1977 to address redlining?

a. Community Reinvestment Act

b. Fair Housing Act

c. Home Mortgage Disclosure Act

d. Equal Credit Opportunity Act

Answer B

Redlining is a process where lenders and when banks refuse to make loans or extend other financial services to minorities and Black communities. The Fair Housing Act was enacted to abolish and ban the practice of redlining.

37. What law does the CFPB enforce?

a. Tax repayment

b. Federal consumer financial laws

c. Disclosure laws

d. Right to recission

Answer B

The Consumer Financial Protection Bureau plays a vital role in the protection of consumers from deceptive lending practices. The agency enforces federal consumer financial laws making sure that all Americans have equal access to the financial markets and that the services are provided in a transparent, fair, and unbiased manner.

38. What is the name of the document created and signed by the lender acknowledging that the borrower has paid off the mortar and the property has no liens?

a. Deed

b. Color of title

c. Satisfaction of mortgage

d. Closing document

Answer C

Once the borrower has paid off the mortgage, the lender will provide the satisfaction of mortgage letter, which will also acknowledge that there are no liens on the property.

39. Which of the following loans does not require mandatory counseling?

a. VA

b. HOEPA

c. HECM (FHA Reverse Mortgage)

d. First-time homebuyers that have a neg amort loan

Answer A

The key aim of the VA home loan program is to assist veterans in financing the purchase of a home. VA loans are available at low-interest rates with favorable terms. No counseling is required for these loans; all high-risk and high-priced loans need counseling.

40. The primary goal of ECOA is to:

a. Eliminate discriminatory lending practices towards all demographics.

b. Ensure that private insurance is canceled when home equity reaches 20%

c. Ensure full disclosures of loans

d. Provide consumers with the ability to cancel a financial contract

Answer A

The key goal of ECOA is to protect American consumers from discrimination based on religion, race, national origin, marital status, gender, religion, or need for public assistance.

41. A homebuyer has just been offered a mortgage that comes with a non-refundable funding fee. What type of loan is he dealing with?

a. VA loan

b. FHA loan

c. USDA loan

d. Jumbo loan

Answer A

In general, VA fees for a mortgage are not refundable, but a lot depends on other features. Those with a service-related disability or lack of knowledge may be able to get a partial refund.

42. What is the name of the clause in the contract which allows the lender to demand full repayment if the borrower defaults on the loan?

a. Acceleration clause

b. Alienation clause

c. Defeasance clause

d. Exculpatory clause

Answer A

Sometimes, the lender may feel that the borrower is going to default on the mortgage, or there may be circumstances where the borrower may not be able to pay the loan. In such cases, the lender can demand immediate payment of the loan before the standard terms on the mortgage have expired. The acceleration clause helps lenders avoid the risk of default by the borrower.

43. What is the name of the clause in the contract which allows the lender to ask for full repayment if the borrower decides to transfer the loan or the home title to another party?

a. Acceleration clause

b. Alienation clause

c. Defeasance clause

d. Exculpatory clause

Answer B

Sometimes the homeowner may decide to transfer the property rights and ownership to a third party. In such scenarios, the alienation clause will come into play- the lender may ask the borrower to first pay off the entire mortgage before the transfer of the property can be done- this is the alienation clause.

44. The letter' X' is used to describe a provision under which Federal Act?

a. RESPA

b. ECOA

c. TILA

d. FACTA

Answer A

Regulation X is a provision of the Securities Exchange Act of 1934. It relates to credit secured both outside and within the United States. Borrowers subjected to Regulation X must prove that the credit they obtained conforms to both Federal Reserve Regulation U (banks) and Regulation T (brokers).

45. A creditor must respond to a payoff request within how many days?

a. 3 days

b. 5 days

c. 7 days

d. 10 days

Answer C

By law, the servicer/creditor is usually required to send a payoff document within seven days of receiving the request.

46. A borrower has several mortgages on his home and was recently given a subordination agreement. What does this mean?

a. That he has two pay both mortgages simultaneously

b. Specifies which mortgage takes precedence

c. Allows him to delay payments on one mortgage

d. He is at liberty to pay on either mortgage

Answer B

When two mortgages are on a property, the subordination agreement specifies which mortgage takes precedence.

47. An appraisal update and completion recertification is also known as?

a. Form 442

b. Form 1000

c. Disclosure form

d. Evidence form

Answer A

Form 442 is a short document that can be used to report an update of an appraisal. The same form is used to document if a new appraisal is warranted.

48. Which of the following is not a protected class of ECOA?

a. Sex

b. Marital status

c. Race

d. Disability

Answer D

In general, ECOA prohibits all types of discrimination, whether it is based on color, race, religion, sex, national origin, marital status, age, or recipient of public assistance. Unfortunately, disability protection does not fall under ECOA.

49. What is a deficiency judgment?

a. Loss of home to foreclosure

b. Lack of judgment when purchasing a home

c. Money awarded to the creditor when assets securing a loan by the debtor do not cover the debt

d. Home awarded to the buyer when the seller rescinds the contract

Answer C

A deficiency judgment is usually a monetary award to creditors when the assets used to secure a loan by the borrower are not enough to cover the debt.

50. What is the FHA reverse mortgage called?

a. Jumbo loan

b. HECM

c. Home equity loan

d. Home equity line of credit

Answer B

The Home Equity Conversion Mortgage (HECM) is the only reverse mortgage insured by the FHA. This particular mortgage is usually available through FHA-approved lenders.

51. What does the abbreviation HPML stand for?

a. High-Priced Mortgage Loan

b. High Productive Money Loan

c. Highest Payout Mortgage Lenders

d. Highest Professional Mortgage lenders

Answer A

A mortgage is considered to be a high-priced mortgage loan (HPML) when the annual percentage rate is a few percentage points greater than the APOR; however, this also depends on the loan type.

52. How many free copies of your credit report can you get from a single credit bureau each year?

a. 1

b. 2

c. 3

d. 4

Answer A

Consumers have the right to request one free copy of their credit report every year. These credit reports can be obtained by contacting any one of the three major consumer reporting agencies (Experian, Equifax, and TransUnion).

53. How many pages is The Closing Disclosure?

a. 2

b. 3

c. 5

d. 7

Answer C

A Closing Disclosure is a short document consisting of five pages. The document is comprehensive and provides in-depth information about the mortgage, the loan terms, the interest rates, projected monthly premiums and all the other costs associated with the loan, including closing costs.

54. What is it called when a document appears to be a legitimate claim of title to a piece of land but, due to a title defect, cannot transfer ownership?

a. Fraud

b. Color of title

c. Fake deed

d. Title defect

Answer B

The color of title refers to an instrument, tool or document that, on the face of it, appears to be a legitimate claim to the property or piece of land. However, a closer look will reveal that there is some type of defect with the title, and hence the property or title cannot be transferred.

55. What is it called when during a real estate transaction, the legal title of the property is being held by a third party until the borrower repays the debt to the lender?

a. Trust deed

b. Security

c. Reconveyance

d. Lien

Answer A

In financial transactions that deal with real estate, sometimes, the legal title of the home or land may be held by a third party- which may be an escrow company, lawyer, bank, or the title company. The third party will hold onto the title until the borrower has made all the payments and has no more debt with the lender. This is known as a trust deed.

56. The Uniform Residential Loan application is also known as form?

a. 1003

b. 1004

c. 1005

d. 1006

Answer A

The Uniform Residential Loan Application is also referred to as the 1003 mortgage application. This is now the standard form that most mortgage lenders use in the United States. The borrower has to complete form 1003 when applying for a mortgage.

57. Which form has been created to report an appraisal of a one-unit property with an accessory building unit in a planned unit development?

a. 1003

b. 1004

c. 1005

d. 1006

Answer B

Form 1004 is designed to make a report of an appraisal of a one-unit property or a one-unit property with an accessory unit as part of a planning unit development.

58. If a potential home buyer wants to know whether the value of the property has changed since a prior approval, what form is usually completed?

a. 442

b. 1003

c. 1005

d. 1009

Answer A

Form 442 is now used to determine if the property value has changed since the initial approval. Form 442 will reveal if the conditions of the first appraisal have been taken into account. Essentially form 442 provides an update on the property value since the initial appraisal.

59. What does TRID stand for?

a. Technology Requirements Integration Division

b. Training Range and Instrumentation

c. Training Requirement Identification Display

d. TILA-RESPA Information Disclosure

Answer D

TRID stands for TILA-RESPA Information Disclosure and is used in real estate to inform people who apply for a mortgage and describe loan lender rules.

60. What is the 30% rule for a mortgage?

a. Homeowner should save 30% of his income each month

b. Homeowners should not spend more than 30% of their gross income on housing

c. A 30% down payment is better than a 20% down payment

d. The mortgage should be 30% of the gross monthly income

Answer B

The general rule in real estate is that homeowners should not spend more than one-third or 30 percent of their gross monthly income on housing. The remaining 70% of the money can be spent on other expenses. Today this is not a realistic rule, as home prices are sky-high.

61. What is the name of the person who promises to pay a borrower's debt in the event the borrower defaults on the loan?

a. Trustee

b. Beneficiary

c. Mortgagee

d. Guarantor

Answer D

Sometimes a borrower may not have the funds to finance a mortgage. In such scenarios, a guarantor may be asked to sign the contract. Hence if the borrower defaults on the mortgage payments, the guarantor is held liable for the money. A guarantor will usually pledge his or her assets as collateral.

62. In real estate, what do the abbreviations HVCC stand for?

a. High-value credit client

b. Home valuation complete code

c. Home valuation code of conduct

d. High-value customer-client

Answer C

The Home Valuation Code of Conduct (HVCC) includes a number of federal guidelines that help make the home appraisal process more reliable. The HVCC prohibits mortgage brokers and real estate agents from selecting or paying appraisers.

63. What is the basic function of the Home Valuation Code of Conduct?

a. Ensure that home inspectors are all licensed

b. Home inspection is done within 30 days of signing the contract

c. Make the home appraisal process more reliable

d. Eliminate fees for the home inspection

Answer C

The Home Valuation Code of Conduct (HVCC) includes a number of federal guidelines that help make the home appraisal process more reliable. The HVCC prohibits mortgage brokers and real estate agents from selecting or paying appraisers.

64. What form does Fannie Mae use to verify the applicant's employment status when applying for a conventional loan?

a. 1003

b. 1004

c. 1005

d. 1006

Answer C

Fannie Mae uses form 1005 to verify the applicant's past and present history of employment.

65. Which form has been created to collect information about the market rent for a single-family property?

a. 1003

b. 1004

c. 1006

d. 1007

Answer D

Form 1007 has been designed to assess the market rent for a single-family unit. The form asks for details on the location, the physical structure of the property, and the terms of the lease.

66. Which form, also known as the Uniform Underwriting and Transmittal Summary, is used by lenders to make underwriting decisions based on the information?

a. 1004

b. 1005

c. 1007

d. 1008

Answer D

Form 1008 by Fannie Mae, also known as the Uniform Underwriting and Transmittal Summary, is often used by lenders to analyze the key summary data of an application and make underwriting decisions based on that.

67. What is the primary function of the Community Reinvestment Act?

a. Prohibit discrimination in lending

b. Ensure everyone can get credit

c. Encourage banks to meet the credit needs of the community

d. Encourage homeowners to buy foreclosed homes

Answer C

The Community Reinvestment Act (CRA) was passed into law in 1977. One of the goals of this act was to encourage and support banks and lenders to meet the credit needs of their community, especially low-income earners.

68. What is it known when a creditor makes a reasonable good faith determination of the borrower's ability to repay a loan?

a. Financial capability

b. ATR/QM rule

c. Good faith rule

d. Earnest money

Answer B

When a creditor makes a reasonable good faith determination of the borrower's ability to repay the loan according to the defined terms, this is known as the Ability-to-Repay/Qualified Mortgage Rule (ATR/QM Rule).

69. Why is underwriting often done in real estate?

a. To determine if the borrower will be at risk for default

b. Determine if the borrower understands the process of home buying

c. Check the personal background of the borrower

d. Check to determine if the lender is offering the right amount of mortgage

Answer A

In the simplest terms, underwriting is a process that determines the risk of a loan. For example, the underwriter will look at the entire financial and credit status of the borrower and determine if he or she is a high or low risk for default. High-risk individuals are usually not offered a loan.

70. What is it called when the defaulting mortgagor's right to prevent foreclosure proceedings on the property and redeem the mortgaged property by discharging the debt seizures by the mortgage within a reasonable time frame?

a. Right of rescission

b. Equitable right of redemption

c. Conveyance

d. Chain of titles

Answer B

There are instances when the borrower has defaulted on the mortgage, but because of the equity of redemption, he or she will try to prevent foreclosure proceedings on the home. At the same time, the borrower will try to redeem the mortgaged property by paying any debt secured by the loan; of course, the equity of redemption only works within a certain period of allocated time.

71. In general, who has the right of redemption of property?

a. The lender

b. The seller

c. The loan officer

d. The borrower

Answer D

Legally the borrower does have the Right of Redemption. Legally the borrower who owns the property is able to reclaim it as long as he or she is able to satisfy a set number of conditions; the primary condition is that the secured loan has to be repaid to prevent foreclosure.

72. What is it called when a broker does not have enough money to fund their own loan but then enters into an agreement with a different lender?

a. Table funding

b. Direct Investing

c. Easement

d. Conveyance

Answer A

When a Broker or Correspondent does not have enough money to fund their own loan but wants to give the appearance that they are a direct lender, they will usually enter into a table funding agreement with a different lender.

73. What is it called when inventory financing involves a loan made by a lender to a company, and the existing inventory is used as collateral?

a. Warehouse funding

b. Bailout scheme

c. Jumbo loan

d. Table funding

Answer A

Warehouse financing is another form of inventory financing. Essentially this type of financing involves a loan made to a manufacturer or company; the company will then transfer all the existing goods or inventory to a warehouse, where it will serve as collateral on the loan.

74. TILA/Regulation Z requires that creditors keep their documentation of compliance for what period of time after the disclosures were made?

a. 3 months

b. 6 months

c. 9 months

d. 24 months

Answer A

Regulation Z recommends that all creditors who refer and/or compensate loan originators maintain their financial and compliance documents for a minimum of 24 months.

75. Prior to any disclosures by the lenders, TILA Regulation permits only one fee from the applicant. What is this fee?

a. Administrative fees

b. Credit check fees

c. Background check fees

d. Fees for the application

Answer B

TILA Reg Z allows only one fee to be collected before disclosures which is the fee for the credit report.

76. The Loan Estimate combines which two documents?

a. Truth in lending and good faith estimate

b. Home loan toolkit and good faith estimate

c. Closing disclosure and home loan toolkit

d. The good faith estimate and the home loan tool kit

Answer A

The document which combines the Truth in Lending Statement required by TILA and the Good Faith Estimate required by RESPA is which of the following:

77. What is the role of section 10 of RESPA?

a. It mandates that all borrowers open an escrow account

b. Limits the amount the borrower is required to deposit into an escrow account

c. Even low-priced loans need an escrow account

d. That the escrow account is held by the lender

Answer B

Section 10 of RESPA has a cap on the amount that a mortgage lender may ask a borrower to place into an escrow account. This money is usually for the private mortgage insurance and property taxes.

78. In general, a complete loan application as per TILA/RESPA consists of how many initial items?

a. 4

b. 6

c. 8

d. 10

Answer B

As per TILA/RESPA, the initial complete loan application consists of the following six pieces of information: Name, Income, Social Security Number, Property Address, Estimated Value of Property, and Mortgage Loan Amount sought.

79. The lender is supposed to provide the borrower the loan estimate document at what

point in time when applying for a loan?

a. Within three days

b. 5 days

c. 7 days

d. 10 days

Answer A

As per the TRID rule, a creditor is responsible for ensuring that a Loan Estimate is delivered to a consumer. This document should be in the mail no later than the third business day after receiving the borrower's "application" for a mortgage loan.

80. The abbreviation TIP is found in the loan estimate form. What does it stand for?

a. Total interest percentage

b. Total investment percentage

c. Timely investment product

d. Thoroughly investigated product

Answer A

The total interest percentage is easily obtained by summing up all of the scheduled interest payments and then dividing the total by the loan amount to get a percentage. The TIP makes one assumption; it assumes that the borrower will make all the monthly payments on time.

81. In general, the new Loan Estimate form does not apply to which of the following:

a. VA loans

b. FHA loans

c. Conventional purchase money loans

d. Mobile home

Answer D

In order to get the Loan Estimate document, one must have the physical address of the property. In general, a loan estimate is not applicable to a mobile home.

82. Today, the Closing Disclosure is a document created from a combination of which of the following:

a. Final Truth in lending and HUD 1 settlement statements

b. Good faith estimate and HUD 1 settlement statement

c. Loan estimate and good faith statement

d. HUD 1 settlement and loan estimate statements

Answer A

The Closing Disclosure is a document that is a combination of the Truth in Lending statement and the HUD-1 Settlement Statement. The Closing Disclosure reflects the actual cost of the mortgage and, in some ways, is similar to the data on the Loan Estimate.

83. The Loan Estimate document is often compared by the borrower with which other document?

a. Closing Disclosure

b. Mortgage servicing Disclosure statement

c. Good faith estimate

d. Sales and Purchase Agreement

Answer A

The borrower is usually given the Loan Estimate, which reveals the approximate monthly payments and closing costs. This document is often compared to the Closing disclosure, which provides the real and final numbers for the loan. The loan Estimate only gives an approximation of the costs.

84. What does consummation mean in real estate?

a. The loan has been approved

b. The Closing is completed

c. The borrower now has a contract with the lender

d. The home appraisal is complete

Answer C

Consummation is said to occur when the borrower/consumer becomes obligated to a financial contract; usually, this contract is with the creditor. In some states, consummation may mean that the borrower has actually signed the mortgage documents.

85. Which person or entity is ultimately responsible for ensuring delivery of the Closing disclosure to the borrower?

a. MLO

b. Mortgage broker

c. Creditor

d. Guarantor

Answer C

While all of these may cooperate in the Closing of the loan, the law holds the creditor ultimately responsible for the content, delivery, and timing of the Closing Disclosure.

86. The first number 3 in the 3-7-3 rule, according to TILA, signifies?

a. Initial disclosure is given three days after the application

b. Closing permitted within three days

c. 3 days to complete the application

d. 3 days to make any edits

Answer A

Initial disclosures are given three business days after receipt of the application, Closing permitted seven business days after that, and an additional three business days wait if corrected disclosures have to be issued.

87. According to TILA, the three days right of rescission is not available for borrowers for which type of loan?

a. Home equity loan

b. Home improvement loan

c. Loans for a vacation home

c. Refinancing personal residence

Answer C

No right of rescission is available for a purchase-money loan on a personal residence or for construction loans, commercial loans, or loans on vacation homes or second homes.

88. According to TILA, creditors must provide how many copies of the Notice of the Right to Rescind?

a. One original

b. Two

c. Triplicate.

d. Five.

Answer B

The law requires two copies that are separate from the sale or credit documents at loan consummation.

89. In general, if the applicant exercises his right to rescind the loan, the creditor must return all funds collected related to the loan within how many days?

a. 5

b. 10

c. 20

d. 30

Answer C

The creditor must return all monies collected within 20 calendar days.

90. Sometimes, TILA allows an extension right of rescission. This extension period is about?

a. 30 days

b. 60 days

c. 365 days

d. 3 years

Answer D

Sometimes the lender or creditor may delay sending the necessary notice and material disclosures; in such scenarios, the borrower or applicant's right to rescind can be extended for up to 3 years.

91. In general, when borrowers are late with the payment, the lender will charge a late fee when the payment is delayed by:

a. 3 days

b. 10 days

c. 15 days

d. 30 days

Answer D

In general, most lenders will charge a late fee when the payment is delayed by 15 days.

92. When a borrower is late with the payments, the lender can charge a maximum late fee of:

a. 1% of the principal and interest payment

b. 5% of principal and interest payment.

c. A flat fee of $1,000

d. Depends on the loan and duration of the delay

Answer B

With most lenders, the grace period for late payments ends after 15 days. At this point, the lender will usually penalize the borrower with a penalty that is 5% of the principal and interest. These penalties can be significant and must be paid ASAP.

93. Which federal agency was created to overcome the problem of identity thefts in real estate?

a. FACTA

b. FCRA

c. FHA

d. FDA

Answer A

The Fair and Accurate Credit Transactions Act (FACTA) was enacted into law by congress in 2003. The major goal of FACTA was to improve protection for customers, especially when it came to identity theft.

94. Which federal agency requires that consumers applying for credit also receive the

home loan Applicant Credit Score information Disclosure notice?

a. FCRA

b. FTC

c. FACTA

d. FDA

Answer C

FACTA recommends that people who apply for credit receive the Home Loan Applicant Credit Score Information Disclosure notice. This document explains in detail their rights.

95. The National Do Not Call Registry does not apply to which of the following?

a. A program that sells goods through interstate phone calls.

b. Telemarketers who solicit consumers on behalf of third-party sellers.

c. Telephone surveyors who seek donations.

d. Non-profit charities

Answer D

There are several exemptions to the Do Not Call registry rules. In general, the Do Not Call rules do not apply to registered and not-for-profit charities.

96. If a borrower discovers that the balance of the loan is markedly greater than it was at the start of the loan process, this type of loan is most likely?

a. Jumbo loan

b. VA loan

c. Negative amortization

d. Compounding loan

Answer C

If the loan continues in a negative amortization status, the balance of the loan will soon be significantly greater than it was at the beginning of the loan. This is because unpaid interest is accruing and is being added to the loan balance.

97. ECOA does not protect against which of the following class of groups?

a. Elderly

b. Minorities

c. Religious

d. Disabled

Answer D

The key goal of ECOA is to protect American consumers from discrimination based on religion, race, national origin, marital status, gender, religion, or need for public assistance.

98. The Fair Housing Act does not protect against which one of the following groups?

a. Elderly

b. Minorities

c. Religious

d. People of different national origin

Answer A

According to The Fair Housing Act, it is illegal to discriminate or harass any individual because of color, race, sex, religion, gender, family status, disability or national origin. There is no protection for elderly under the Fair Housing Act.

99. To combat redlining, the federal government passed which Act in 1977?

a. ECOA

b. Homeowners Protection act

c. Fair Credit Reporting act

d. Community Reinvestment act

Answer D

The Community Reinvestment Act of 1977 was passed into law to first and foremost address the issue of redlining; this was an illegal practice by lenders who denied services and credit to certain people living in some areas of a city. Today, redlining is considered illegal and discriminatory.

100. Which of the following federal laws is considered to be an Anti-Predatory Lending Law:

a. USDA

b. HOEPA

c. FCRA

d. FACTA

Answer B

Yes, the Home Ownership and Equity Protection Act is designed to prevent lenders from heaping additional costs and penalties on top of an already high-cost loan.

Made in the USA
Las Vegas, NV
07 November 2023

80398369R00179